What encourag[...]
i[...] all p[...]

The Ring
of Words

Poems from

The Daily Telegraph

Arvon International Poetry
Competition 1998
in association with
Duncan Lawrie Limited

Introduction by ANDREW MOTION

Love
Amy xxx

SUTTON PUBLISHING

23 September '98

First published in 1998 by
Sutton Publishing Limited · Phoenix Mill
Thrupp · Stroud · Gloucestershire · GL5 2BU

British Library Cataloguing in Publication Data
A catalogue record for this book is available from the British
Library

ISBN 0 7509 1981 7

Typeset in 11pt Garamond.
Typesetting and origination by
Sutton Publishing Limited.
Printed in Great Britain by
Butler & Tanner, Frome, Somerset.

Contents

CONTENTS

The Daily Telegraph Arvon International
Poetry Competition 1998
in association with
Duncan Lawrie Limited

Prizes

The Daily Telegraph Prize (Winner) of £5,000
5 Duncan Lawrie Prizes (Runners-up) of £500 each
10 Duncan Lawrie Prizes (Highly Commended) of £250
each

Judges

Fleur Adcock, Grey Gowrie,
Charles Moore, Andrew Motion.

The Arvon Foundation gratefully acknowledges the sponsorship
of The Daily Telegraph and Duncan Lawrie Limited.

Introduction

ANDREW MOTION

Here's a disagreeable truth: if you meet the judge of a literary prize when he or she is in the middle of the process, you're sure to get an earful of complaints. There are a horrendous number of entries. The standard is dreadful. The fellow-judges are biased or deranged. Never mind the fact that everyone knew what was entailed when they signed up. Never mind, either, that everyone on the admin. side is being paid. The fact is: there's something about judging which encourages moaning. And that something has got a lot to do with temporary superiority ('I'm above all this really – and beyond it, as well'), and with a weird kind of relief ('If I were a contestant I'd probably get nowhere; this way, there's a guaranteed fee and my name all over the place').

All of which means: any one involved in judging this year's *Daily Telegraph*/Arvon prize would do themselves a simple favour if they said they'd enjoyed themselves, and agreed that those who didn't win had at least put their entrance fee towards a good cause.

As it happens, none of this presents any problems. To take the good cause element first. The Arvon Foundation is now thoroughly well established as the best organiser of writing courses in Britain. Week in, week out, writers of all kinds and varying abilities meet at its three centres, and find a wonderful mixture of space, solitude and society. In addition, they get a dose of professional advice – about how to burnish what they've already done, about how to stretch for what lies just beyond their reach, and about how to make remote dreams become obtainable. All in all, the centres do a really extraordinary amount of good – for writers and writing in particular, and for cultural life in general.

Now to the pleasures of judging. I wouldn't be telling the whole truth if I didn't admit to quailing a little when, one evening earlier this summer, I opened my front door and saw my share of the poems for the first time. Even though they had been tidied into folders (I got eighteen), these folders were thick, they were overpoweringly red, they were heavy, they were swollen at the spines . . . Still, I soon had a reason for keeping my feelings to myself. 'What's that, Dad?', my children wanted to know, as I made a stack in a corner of my study. 'Oh, poems.' 'What, *all* of it?' 'Mmmmmn.' There was simply no answer to that, or not one they thought suitable for my ears. As for me, I knew that if I showed any flicker of disquiet, I'd loosen their already precarious grip on the delights of reading.

When it came to starting, I remembered at once why I had been pleased to be approached in the first place. A competition like the Arvon is more than just a trawl through the desks and notebooks of many thousands of writers. It is a kind of enormous literature-survey as well. And as my reading continued over the next several weeks, I found a part of my mind that wasn't fully occupied with the business of weighing and evaluating was silently drawing up a list of questions, posed by what was passing in front of my eyes.

It went something like this. *How does American poetry differ from British poetry?* It's always better typed and generally more sombre – in an irony-free sense. *Are there any obviously recurring subjects?* God yes: love of places, love of loved ones, death of loved ones, death of Princess Diana. *Are there any prevailingly strong influences?* Difficult to tell. The strongest pull was exercised by a mish-mash of the mighty dead, rather than any one or two contemporaries. *What's the state of play, broadly speaking, about form?* The Brits are much more orthodox than the Americans, but even across the Atlantic the Modernist legacy seems to have dwindled to almost nothing at least among people who enter competitions.

Inevitably, there are some disturbing conclusions to be drawn here. To put them bluntly (and to risk making that superior/relieved moan): the submission contained a great many poems written by people who obviously put out a lot but took in very little, who thought that good writing and good reading were not connected, whose aesthetic ideas had been shaped when they first read the Georgians and never challenged since, and who were not interested in finding out how their pastoral/lyric world might be adapted to include things that were urban/political/rough-edged. Many of these offerings, indeed, seemed to me hardly poems at all (no shape, no rhyme, no subject) – which left me feeling puzzled as to why they'd been cast as such in the first place. The lure of 'being a poet'? Or sheer incompetence?

On the other hand – as this anthology proves – there were also plenty of times when elaborate schemes were expertly realised, when forms and subjects became happily married, when ambitions were stretched and achieved. And also plenty of other times when, within less 'professional' and attention-seeking creations, the efforts of watchfulness, patience, pondering and plain honesty were handsomely rewarded. All this made the experience of judging a continually exciting one: each new poem represented a new and self-contained world, in which anything might happen.

Which leads to another thing. However tight the range, however narrow the mood, the cumulative effect of so many poems about landscape, love and loss was to redefine an enduring truth about poetry. Poets can be as clever, difficult, socially engaged and politically wired as maybe, but it does poetry itself a disservice if we ignore its value as a primitive emotional release. Of course not all the work entered for this competition had organised itself adequately, and of course the language/rhythm/form of others was dull. But the big pulse-beat was there all the same – throughout. In its complicated way, this made the whole experience of judging feel moving.

Readers of the anthology will form their own view about the wisdom or otherwise of the judges' decisions. That is as it should be. We had our formal job to do; readers now have their less formal one – the one that allows literature to stay alive when it is away from competitions and campuses. When my own poem 'The Letter' won the first Arvon Prize, I told myself the only sensible thing to do was consider myself lucky, admit my good fortune, and try to write better in the future. I knew that if my poem was to have a life, it would have to be elsewhere.

And now all the poems in this book are beginning their after-life. Being one of their first readers was a great pleasure; I hope that all those who come to them next will share that pleasure – in the true heartlands.

Technical Assistance

The President is sitting in the garden of the palace
surrounded by his extended family – wife,
cousins, nieces, several uncles
by marriage, and a personal bodyguard
in American fatigues carrying
Kalashnikov automatic rifles.

The lawns are green and well cut
with bougainvillaea along the borders.
In the centre of the lawn is a large tree,
a Cedar of Lebanon, which provides shade
and respite from the sun. It is famously known,
and featured on stamps, as 'The President's Tree'.

Apart from the soldiers and servants, I
am the only man in the palace garden
without a tie. It is five o'clock
in the afternoon and still very hot.
I am waiting to be asked to present myself
officially to the President under the tree.

Two hours ago it seemed perfectly
reasonable to wear my light grey
tropical suit, open at the neck,
spotless, almost new and certainly
well-pressed. That was,
as it turned out, an error of judgement.

Although not desperately serious
(no socks would have been suicidal),
my offence is an affront to the President
and to the occasion, and cannot therefore
go unpunished. 'Tieless in Gaza',
I mutter, sweating under the hot sun.

The visitors – all except me,
that is – have now been presented
to the President, and are standing around chatting
in the shade of the President's Tree.
I can hear the President explaining: '*Psalms* . . .
104, you know . . . Cedars of Libanus.'

I have met the President several times
already. He knows me as the newly appointed
Advisor for Fine Arts and Museums –
'on loan from London' is his way
of putting it; but I have not yet been
formally presented at a President's reception.

Tea is being served in the deep
cool shade of the tree (milk
or lemon, Madam?), there are thinly-cut
cucumber sandwiches. And suddenly
I am noticed, ushered in from the heat
to the presence of His Excellency.

He smiles apologies – he hadn't realised
I was there as a guest. '*You are so familiar –
like an Old Master, already known
before encountered.*' I am the ancien
régime discredited. '*Please mention
my Degas to the French Ambassador,*' he says.

The guests assume I am one of the household,
an intimate in casual dress, just in
from the hills, perhaps. The family, extended
under the Cedar tree, believes
I am an esoteric freak. In London
I am registered as Technical Assistance.

I mingle with the guests, but clearly
am not accepted as one of them (no tie
must, after all, mean something).
'This tree' I am asked by a couple –
handsome, pleasantly seductive – *'surely it was here long
before Independence?'*

They are English, holding on to a memory
of Empire and fair play. The invitation
is clear: recognition, complicity, guile,
and a sporting option on betrayal.
Let's just, their faces smile, at least
agree on history and the true facts.

I am, I suppose, a guardian of history
and the true facts: *'Ah yes'*, I reply,
'but you see, the President has given trees status –
it's our new conservation policy' –
*the best I can do, tieless in Africa,
at the end of a long century.*

B.A. HUMAR

Above Suilven

I.M. NORMAN MacCAIG

Scotsman speaking at my shoulder, I've
tagged a longish way behind you on
so many journeys, tramping through the shining
corries, or diving like a guillemot
into that sea all made with words.

I knelt and tied your shoes for you
one morning in a morning-after kitchen
while you sat fastened into age
like something borrowed to look haughty in.

You said you wrote your poems straight
onto the page and let them stand.
Still at your feet, I don't believe you, but
you surely made the swerving wit seem easy
an Englishman can't somehow manage.

Norman, I'll say goodbye. I'm heading North
to look out for your star above Suilven,
your favourite mountain. Goodbye again.
You wouldn't want to find me sentimental.

PETER BENNET

América

FOR RIGOBERTA MENCHU
AND LA COMUNIDAD NUEVA ESPERANZA,
EL SALVADOR

All the earth is a grave and nothing escapes it;
nothing is so perfect that it does not descend to its tomb . . .
Filled are the bowels of the earth with pestilential dust
once flesh and bone, once animate bodies of men
who sat upon thrones, decided cases, presided in council,
commanded armies, conquered provinces,
possessed treasure, destroyed temples,
exalted in their pride, majesty, fortune, praise, power.
Vanished are these glories, just as the fearful smoke
    vanishes
that belches forth from the infernal fires of Popocatepetl.
Nothing recalls them but the written page.

                    Hungry-Coyote (Netzahualcoyotl)
                          King of Texcoco 1431–72

RETURN TO EL MOZOTE

Expert diggers of the dead are brushing bones,
their pit protected from the sun by canvas
stretched across a skeleton of wooden slats.
We reach a metal shape that holds a plaque
assuring us THEY DID NOT DIE; THEY ARE WITH US
AND ALL HUMANITY, a silhouette of a family,

a monument that stands beneath a cross on stones
where I think the village chapel used to be
before we burned it down and hid the dead.
Some cows chewing thistles rest in shade.

Days before we mowed them down we warned
the peasants to move. They said they hadn't helped
the guerrillas, gave us soup and a supply of corn
for the whole battalion, thought they'd not be hurt,
being Protestants, odd ones out in Morazán –
'balanced like beams across the shoulders of the war,'
the pastor told us, smiling – and so they stayed.
The jefe knew a bluff when he heard one but played
a waiting game while the neighbouring villages fled.
Then, near Christmas, we struck; and hid the dead.

The Truth Commission men walk round the grave.
I'm told to get the jeep; I salute and leave.
One survived who heard her children plead
but bit her tongue and hid in thorns and knew
she was the one who'd been chosen to tell the truth
which is there, unearthed, the evidence amnesties
and Peace Accords will bury. THEY DID NOT DIE;
THEY ARE WITH US – I laugh and shake the keys
and kick the crowns off thistles. The truth? It lies.
There. On the tongues of lazy cattle under trees.

THE BOOK OF THE PEOPLE

A Spanish priest translates the Popol Vuh
and catches fever. The words mutate and snake
across the page like smoke; twenty voices

chant the secret Quauhtlemallan legends
from between the covers which have turned to bark.

RIGOBERTA'S FIRST VISIT TO THE CITY

With your humble, starving father you sold willow.
You saw him bow in offices to puffed-up men
who peered from machines that tapped words on wood,
square tortillas streaked with beans of ink.

The rest of the week you trekked the unknown streets
like the time in the woods when your dog ran away, too
    hungry
to lead you home, and you'd nothing but twigs to chew.

Your father bought you ice he couldn't afford,
its numbness a mystery hunger couldn't ruin.
All the way home in the covered truck, penniless
and gaunt, you slept, dreaming of typewriters and snow.

THE WOODEN MEN ARE BANISHED

Before the maize-paste was human-shaped
the men of wood were kings and ruled badly.

One day, everything got its revenge.

The small animals and the large animals,
the earthen jars and griddles,
the plates and pots and grinding stones,
all rose up and spoke
and smacked the faces of the wooden men.

Treat us like this and we'll rip you to shreds
they said as they ripped them to shreds.

The stones of the fire exclaimed,
You built us up and cooked on us!

The griddles and pots shouted,
You put us on the fire and blackened us!

The houses bellowed,
You lived in us and warmed in us!

Then all together,
And you didn't even ask our permission!

THE SEASONS

The heat beats down in both the wet and dry
on Usulutan's southern coastal plain.
Its sound is the insects' pitch, the constant cry
that buzzes in the air and raps the ear with pain.
In the drought, the dust, a packet-mix
for later rain to soup, obscures the land.
Pot-holed water traps the village trucks
like armadillos when malaria, hatched in these ponds,
arrives with the rain; green erupts from the dust
and corn pokes its fingers through the ground
reaching up for men to snap its wrists.
At night the lightning revives the rusty land
where nature delicately holds the reasons
for suffering this weather and these seasons.

SAN SIMON

Good Friday has come and I'm in the square,
rum in my pocket, the sun in my hair.
The crowds throw candles and offer me cigars;
the church is empty and so are the bars
for everyone has come to pray for my grace,
even Mary and her Son who take second place
to me, San Simón, who leads the parade
without any fuss or a priest's masquerade.

Soon I'll be burned in someone's back-yard,
away from the church where now I'm on guard –
the Son needs his moment – but I'll rise again
and be saved for a year in the brotherhood of men
who know the work of saints is hidden from their eyes
deeper in the earth than the height of the skies.

FLOOD

When the Lempa burst we camped in the cattle-shed,
our highest point. The pigs bumped their heads
and chewed the strings on the over-loaded hammocks
where the children sat as the rising water swilled.
The rain stopped when darkness fell but we watched
our backs and slept in shifts and dreamt we drifted
to a foreign land. The morning sun lifted
nothing of the water, which clutched our thighs and pulled.

I knew the crops were lost and in the end
cholera would come, but the only time I cared

was when a tarantula thought Maria was land
and climbed her leg, and she, too tired to be scared,
calmly plucked it in the dark brown sauce
which trailed its bubbles in a perfect line of dots.

THE DISAPPEARING ACT

The boys, disguised as conjurors, went to the court
of the arrogant lords and drew crowds with tricks.

They took a dog and hacked it to bits
and when the final limb was chopped
the dog was whole. The lords came up
and told the boys to kill a servant.

The machetes swung but the scattered limbs re-formed
and the man was alive and stronger than before.

The lords were amazed and said, *Now you!*
The boys showered themselves with blows
and drenched the grass with gore. Like a dream
they appeared as before and the grass was clean.

The arrogant lords could not resist: *Kill us
but keep us alive!* The boys did the job. And paused.

The crowd waited for the resurrected
to move but the limbs just lay and bled
and the severed heads just lay and stared
at nothing and the boys just vanished in the wind.

LANGUAGE SCHOOL OUTING, QUETZALTENANGO

The Tutor

I love to show the gringo college kids
the graves; I always stop at the wall that divides
the marble tombs of those who bought their bliss
from the mounds where babies lie unbaptised.
I tell them about the disappeared and say
at least these dead have crosses at their heads.
I love how reactions change: tears all day,
then questions on how the formal imperative ends.

The Student

I know about these crimes, but who can I blame?
He thinks we're innocents abroad and he's got
all the answers, but would he, if he asked the same
question, point the finger to this very spot?
Who fully blames his own? We're all, at best,
tourists of the dead who have no final rest.

THE FIELD OF REEDS

The hawk vomited the snake;
the snake vomited the toad;
the toad couldn't vomit
for the louse stuck in its throat.

The priest looks up from the page.
He knows he sees the future
and his eyes have the fury of a saint's.

11

He sees five hundred years
of a people choking those
who would swallow them up; he knows
the message of their heroes
will fly beyond the page
just as the reeds will grow
which the boys planted
in the middle of their home
saying, *Do not weep,*
mother, for here we leave
the sign of our fate.

ALLAN CROSBIE

Great Grandfather

Your son, nine, works
in the barber shop, sweeping hair from the floor,

stirring lather in small heavy bowls.
You are proud of this. Next year

he will leave school, and begin
being paid for his work.

You save to buy him the tools
of his trade: metal combs,

scissors (one long and one short),
razor with a first set of blades.

It is a good thing to work indoors
and not in the fields.

It is a good thing to work in daylight
and not in the mines.

In your house, by the front door
hangs a shaving mirror,

its silver worn half away,
but in the barber shop

your son polishes a mirror
so perfect it is invisible.

In it, your son can see himself
from head to knees.

The white starched apron covers him
to the tops of his shoes,

your firstborn, the one
who always climbed from his bed.

You had to tie the hem of his nightgown
to the bed post, so he would not wander.

No fear of the dark, your son crawled
through the night hallway,

miner's son, and only you would hear him,
his hand-pats on the floor

like water dripping through a fault.

SUZANNE CLEARY

Professor

In my study of female circumcision
amongst the Sudanese tribes,
it has been interesting to note
that the procedure has no noticeable effect
on subsequent marriage and child-bearing,
and that few side-effects trouble the patient.
Indeed, it would seem that the women themselves
champion the practice, or so I gather
when I am able to talk to them,
which is not often,
owing to the various tribes' particular codes of conduct
which I am loath to break.
However, I have asked women to describe the procedure –
the knife, the needle, the sutures, the aftercare –
not because I take pleasure
in hearing about such things (needless to say)
but because there isn't the pain you'd expect.
They just go numb

and their spirits leave them,
racing in herds across the plains,
trampling the dust of the plains
and disappearing over the edge of the world.

EVA SALZMAN

Remembering the Future

He will have to be quiet so he will go and sit
in the old armchair in the corner and look at
one of his Dad's books about the war.

This one will be about the Eighth Army
in the desert. There will be pictures of tank battles
at night which will look like the time his Dad

spilt white paint on the pavement
but his favourite part will be right at the end
where it shows you all different types

of desert. How ever many times he looks
he will never believe it's not just all sand.
The book will slip off his lap and his Dad

will say 'Put it down' so he'll get his own book,
probably *Look and Learn* or *World of
Knowledge*. The war will be in there, too,

a story about a young man from a tiny village
who wants to be a painter but has to go
and fight when all his friends get killed.

He is a tank driver and helps win a battle
but loses an arm. In the last frame, he will be
a famous painter, one sleeve pinned up,

painting pictures about the war and the tanks
that make other men cry. Over the page,
there will be another story, in colour this time,

about what the boy's life is going to be like
at the end of the century. Young men,
looking like the painter in the other story,

will walk about smoking pipes in enormous domes.
or travel on monorails between buildings
that will be several hundred storeys high.

All the world will be just one country.
It will be a wet Saturday afternoon
somewhere in the late nineteen-sixties.

An Airfix kit of a Lancaster bomber
his Dad'd said he'd help with will not be getting built.
Wingless, it will lie on the dining room table.

DAVID KENNEDY

Maxwell's Rainbow

*— the electromagnetic spectrum, from short to long wavelength:
gamma rays, x-rays, ultraviolet, visible light, infrared and radio.*

GAMMA RAYS

No substance
Just a sly
downpour
from the sky

an uncommon
vibration
you can't see,
quicksilver
as the gap

between what's said
and what's meant
but then it's gone
and you can't ever
put your finger on it.

Such gauzy
stuff can't break
our bones but it does
make changes
in DNA:

the story
of the first ever
corkscrew willow
found growing
outside Hiroshima;

the odds for
and against misshapes
or being the wrong
side of statistics;

the nature of sickness,
how it starts years
before you know.

X-RAYS

That film of a right hand
playing the piano,
its macabre grace
revealed to the naked eye
as blackened bones
and a wedding ring

as though it had passed
through fire and all
that's left were the bare
bones and the foggy
outline of arpeggios
articulating themselves.

ULTRAVIOLET

At the end of winter my blue-eyed,
fair-skinned friend is down in the dumps.
Sad. He can't explain why, he just is,
huddles close as he can to his lightbox,
watching the skyline glow through all
the luminous spaces of the copper beech
and waiting for the days to lengthen.

By midsummer he's sunbathing
and looking out through sunspecs.
Too much exposure irritates
his northern skin, spills straight
to the basal layers of his animal fears

till his hairs rise up on end, but taking
the glasses off doesn't restore anything
because, for a minute or so, the garden
is much brighter than it should be.

VISIBLE LIGHT

Last night a friend died and something came undone,
like a hole softly opening in the ozone layer
or the vague unease of an unglazed window.

And so today the world is less safe than it was yesterday,
more sad and mysterious, but even while I'm wondering
if I live my own life well enough, the moon comes full,

daffodils stand unearthly in it and when a moth dives into
my headlamps on the way home, it is a short-lived fleck
of light, whose sudden life is a basic property of night.

INFRARED

Mid-morning and my cat's outside on his back in the sun,
limbs splayed out and letting go, eyes shut and I swear it
smiling, on the first, malnourished day of spring.

The earth's warming up like a stone, the expansion
of elements happening smoothly as if the entire planet
were taking up more room and its core smells different,
the skin of the earth giving way, unfastening and letting
things through as though an underworld were swelling
up through this one, the unseen bald white tips
of it crashing through into ours and growing green.

And we love it, lay ourselves flat on the grass
and soak up the sun, having the best of both worlds
and leaving heat maps on the ground after dark
on those rare summer days and nights that are close
as we get to any real evidence for a warm-blooded heart.

RADIO

Long ripples coming in, enough time between each crest to
    turn over, fall
asleep, and sink down past . . . 2 am . . . 3 am . . . 4 . . .
    plenty of time to dream an
ocean with wide-winged birds slanting and sliding beneath
    undulating skies

and coils of seaweed lowering and lifting in a half-hearted
    tide. . . time to
listen for the belly flop of water slapping at fat stones or
    watch the way
the water sparkles, slowly, how the mist comes, everyone
    dreaming
or dreamed of through a drift of fog across unknown waters
    . . . everything
muffled, nothing clear, yet hearing from a long way off, the
    limbic pulse of
the self's long loop around the world, every single
    morning, something in you
making the choice between coming back or staying always
    on the other side.

DIANA SYDER

The Grand Public Deflation

Midnight, and the white castle's time has come.
Under floodlights, the seams are ripped open –
cold, plasticky air stings our faces,
crenellations flop like loose milk-teeth,
the four turrets loll inwards like drunk friends.

And just in time, between the collapsing portals,
out float three be-wimpled, be-girdled, gauzy Ladies,
each holding a large needle, strong thread
and a little silver knife.
They hover, and the first Lady speaks:

For all this time we Ladies
have been practising by the fire-side,
on squares of shaven, pierced, slit boar-skin,
prepared for us in the kitchens
and brought up on covered trays.

Now we can visit the battlefield
where lie our fallen men,
and on them, at last,
we shall display our skills.

They glide over the subsiding drawbridge
(the crowd parting) and down the path
that threads through dark trees
into farmland.

CAROLINE FRANKLYN

Garden Party

The flowers are out.
Carnations' frilly lips
lipsticked pink, white tu-tus
starched. Heavily kohl'd,
sooty poppy eyes druggily
smudged under droopy red
lids old necked creped
promise exotic pleasure.
Sinatra-eyed Forget-Me-
Nots twinkle, Love-in-a
Mists' Seventies revival
Abba shadow bright blue,
how the old roses nodding
in the corner in their antique
shades of dusty white petticoats,
flouncy frocks in fading wine
taffeta, hard red old lady lips
pursed at the centre, disapprove.
Lilies, covered heads bowed
like wimpled nuns in fitting
white bride gowns, they love.
And fat purple velvet-dressed
pansies demure as Victorian
royalty curtseying.

They are waiting to be asked
to dance, trying hard as schoolgirls,
wishing the wind in their skirts,

to whirl until their heads a blur
in the blue sky, drinking sun
into sweetly liquored throats.

Clenched tense as fists – *we're
hardly ever welcome* – weedy
fingers open from thin wrists
in earth. The grass is stoned,
flat out; it thinks the sparkle
of daisies pinned to its chest
are stars floated down. Morning
Glory thinks it can fly, climbing
in its blue bell sleeves to the house's
highest eye with balcony lid.

All afternoon, it's a garden party.
They want to lift their rooted foot
like monkeys' tails in air, losing
the plot. Even the most cultured
flowers, the tender hot-house plants,
the delicate in-bred, are wild. As if
nature's ever young exuberant
green gods have slipped from woods
and hills uninvited over the wall,
gate-crashed, bringing their loud
flower music, and lush summer frenzy.

GILLIAN FERGUSON

Driving to Stoke Poges

she is stowed in the back of the Daimler
encased in metal which cushions will not soften
the callipers grip her leg
her corset digging in, giving her gyp
her steel-tipped stick nudges her on every bend

her husband drives badly: he does it on purpose
he swears and snarls above the engine
crouched forward, furious, as if caged

their nephew is hunched against the door
shying away from the pounce on the gear-stick
the snatch at the brake: his bare legs look cold

they are driving to Stoke Poges for the boy's benefit
it will take him out of himself
last weekend it was Bekonscot
before that Hatfield House
he is quiet as a mouse
but unbearably polite

she notices he turns his head to the side
taking in every lane, each suburban garden
glimpsing the blossom between the beeches

she takes a cigarette and closing her eyes
braces herself for every breath
she thinks of distances travelled
destinations unreached

lunch did not go down well
this motoring is indigestible
afternoon tea at Eton will choke them all

she prays for a collision with one fatality
headstones piled up under the yews
the churchyard scorched, flowers soured with oil

she exhales white fire
passing clouds

decades later
I stand under the canopy of the lych-gate
a faint smell of bonfire in the air

nothing is quite as I remember it
the spaces are greater, the shadows shorter
there is nobody
around whom I must negotiate

I am talking about the journey

GORDON SIMMS

The Snowman's Chronicle

i
My maker rubbed his cold hands.
He named me Caedmon and said,
'Sing about the beginning of created things',
but I knew only the lies of poetry.

It was afternoon,
an old woman returned my smile
and came back fumbling with a camera
to squint at the picture in its frame –
a snowman, a damson tree and blue sky.

When mothers pointed up at me
I was Jesus to the little children.

There was a quiet time,
aeroplane trails melted across early stars,
my sweat froze,
the bird-bath changed into a moon
and I was happy
watching my maker and his woman
making preparations in lighted rooms.

I sang to myself
about the sudden brilliance of garden lights
and warm people received at the door
shuffling salt-and-sand into the mats,
reappearing in the conservatory,

the dining-room,
the conservatory.
I sang their elegance

until a doorway shone,
('The Death of Chatterton' on the wall)
and one walked towards me
carrying silver shoes.
She melted my lips and strutted back
to laughter and applause.

After the lights went out
I dreamt I was a Green Man:

a gardener was mowing round me
and a goldfish with moss rested on my shoulder
as I looked at the sky through damson blossom
but a gritting-lorry woke me,
flicking yellow strobe-light left and right

and when I woke again
the sky was great crumbs of snow
and I started singing.

ii
The milkman whistled his one tune,
'Around the world I searched for you',
the post arrived and newspapers.

I was alone in my element
counting the chimneys with smoke.

The curtains opened. He called her
and they looked down, amused by me
or the two collared-doves pecking at ice.

A tractor with nine bales of hay.

Opposite, a woman carrying a kettle
footprinted her lawn to the birdbath,
detached a convex lens
and placed it on the snow.
'And how are all your gifted pupils, Miss Lockwood?'

Logs of ash, apple and oak
and on top, unsolicited,
holly and mistletoe.

The church clock
struck all the wrong hours
then twelve.

The sun gave me a shadow.

When the house wore holly
they remembered me.
I was completed with a crown
and the two gloved hands
pressed it down.

Radio Malvern from an electrician's van:
Barbara calling from Barnard's Green
with anagrams from the name, 'Elgar' –
Glare, Large, Regal and Lager.
'Grael' was disallowed by Mike
on Sue's advice.

Children home from school
lit rooms with TV and computer screens.

The priest of the gritting-lorry
performed his ritual.
At a safe distance
a new car was driven home
to a house thatched with snow
and fringed with icicles,
to a sparkling Christmas tree
and a red-ribboned wreath on the door,
to a cocktail cabinet,
to her and them.

Under the constellations I dreamt
I was a poet in a summer-house
with a view of blossoms
and a lane to a farm on the hill.
The traffic was cider and milk
and a livestock transporter
with human faces peering out.
I wrote with black ink on black paper.

Two drunks woke me, 'Bleed, you bastard',
throwing railings as javelins
which landed short and wide
and I was forgotten.
Still pissing, one fell forward,
'Who fuckin' pushed me?'
A fight,
a sentimental reconciliation:
'Listen, brothers got to stick together.
You remember, whatever fuckin' happens,

you always got a brother.
Oi, you fuckin' listenin' to me?'
'Do you mean it?'

The telephone box
attracted a cold man
and became his room for the night.

iii
After breakfast from a suitcase
he faced the traffic
with a word on cardboard
strung round his neck –
SOUTHAMPTON.

The gate creaked on two notes
for 'Around the world',
for letters and newspapers.
The air became fragrant with breakfasts.
Chimneys flourished.

Eleven o'clock.
Ice falling from the walnut tree
was imitated everywhere.

Rain.

Radiant umbrellas.

Rain growing on the damson tree
ripened quickly and tortured me.

Avalanches exposed all the roofs,
their browns and greys
tinted with lichens.

Grass.

Remember,
I, Caedmon, once sang.

GEOFFREY MASON

Expatriate

Somewhere between the sea and the dark blue devil
my grin combines the contented smile of a man entirely
successful in a nine-house hamlet on an island
in the Inland Sea, and the faded snarl of a willing exile.

I sit in a rotting rattan rocking chair playing with
words like that in steaming inertia and nursing
the brown music of the spheres in the expanding
paunch of my universe. I've discovered perspiration
and chopped onions have the same smell,
like me, somehow intensely likeable.

Middle-age, it seems, is a lazy touch-and-go race between
the windblown charisma of a white mane and absolute
sunblazed baldness, ending in a draw: one perfectly
    groomed
grey hair. Mirrors tell me better than vernacular
    newspapers
all I need to know about the changing face of the world.

My wooden house is like a museum in a provincial town
nobody visits: full of working clocks, British souvenirs,
used pewter ashtrays, dragons, statues of heathen gods;
a mildewed ship loaded with textbooks permanently out of
    print.

I swim in the beautiful black waters of my students' eyes:
it is my business to excite them with the glamorous

calibres of language, and to teach them how to say
Good morning ten thousand times without me or them
once sounding tired, and with perfect intonation.

People here repeatedly ask me the difference between
words like *maybe* and *perhaps*, and I can't answer,
possibly because we probably never really understand
the language we speak. And when I visit England,
people on trains think I come from Russia, so often in fact
that I imagine I really was born somewhere beyond
Samarkand. But it's more liberating to walk, irresponsibly
alien, through my village birthplace in the Midland hills.

I feel now like a kind of kingpin in a foreign court,
but a soothsaying friend once told me I would die
falling ablaze from a great height. I'm extra
careful when I travel by air, but there's so little
a man can do. My strongest hope is that whenever
it's going to happen, not too many people will be hurt
in the huge earthquake I'm convinced will occur
a few days before my outlandish funeral.

GAVIN BANTOCK

Upturn

My father at the front window
on a drizzled July Sunday
following a speck of orange
snail's-pace across the bay –
too small to be of any matter.

Never at his best on a Sunday
he would fidget from Mass to tea-time
jingling change in the pocket
of a dark blue suit, adjusting
the radiogram to Athlone.

He'd check again on and off.
Only when it was lost
to sight beyond the headland
did he knock on a neighbour's door.
They had the boat out in minutes.

And found the men in time
gripping an upturned hull.
Their arms and hands were numb
and would be for weeks –
the paper said next day.

Sundays went on the same,
my father restless, jingling,
keeping a watch on the open sea.

ANNE-MARIE FYFE

The Singer

In the photograph on the back cover
of the singer's first disc for seven years
he looks out through a rain-streaked window –
one half of his face,
blurred, smiles; the other,
troubled, is clear. He's turning away

slightly, as if to turn away
from himself. If you cover
one side of a photograph, then the other,
you sometimes see two people, years
of differences between them, the face
like hills at dawn from the window

of a plane. The singer leans on the window-
sill, awkward, staring. You look away,
recognising in the expression on his face
how imperfectly you can ever cover
the actual with the imagined self, despite years
of acting naturally: slips of the tongue, other

turns of phrase, add up to another
story. Through the shop window
an unfamiliar city lights up. For years
you stayed; how many went away
before you began to discover
you needed the same? And had to face

admitting that one side of your face
was deep in debt to the other,
that cantilevered promises could never cover
the distance from harbour window
to the view itself, a world away.
The singer's gaze surprises: the years

you loved his songs for their innocence were the years
you believed in your own; now his face
says: Everything can be taken away.
One bright eye resembles the shaded other
but neither is the window
of the soul; the glance is finally opaque, a cover-

ing. And the soul? Watch the face of another
watching you, for years; there's a chance you'll discover,
singly, or together (and it will be worth it) a way to open
   the window.

ANDREW JOHNSTON

The Glass-Blower

A month after the miscarriage,
we watch a glass-blower
fill himself full of puff
and breathe life into dead space.

A bubble pullulates from a knot,
a hot celestial drop,
into a gaseous envelope,
a molten clotted globe,
enjoying its buoyancy,
sustaining its miracle of self-belief,
until its wobbling elongating film
grows taut as a raindrop
in its transparent caul.

The room grows smaller and smaller
as the limpid bubble's membranous sac
stretches clear to the ceiling,
staggering elastically
as it lengthens and cools.

I imagine for a moment
all the vitreous flasks
breaking through the wall,
floating free and letting fall
a host of glaucous bubbles –
hovering over the city like
swarms of soapy cherubim,

clinging airily to
the surface of the river
then popping one after another
like the souls which
make themselves known at night
as drops of water,
distilling at the warm touch of a face.

And if one definition of an angel
is that it takes up no space,
 then you were blessed:
a luminous trace in the memory.

The touch of fingers in
the dark and silence –
undiscovered,
unknowable, unnamed.

CHRIS GREENHALGH

The Story

It needed to be simpler so I told it again

Folk are used to exaggerated talk of moons
so I placed the moon accurately,
said to look at it, it's eight feet below
that telephone pole
just between the points
of the white fir, the blue spruce,
if distances are as they seem
But they'd seen too many moons and were bored
So I told it again

We're surrounded by lies I said,
and installed as correctly as I could
the town hall and gibbets of flagpoles
I put the people and their families in small red houses
with double glazing so clear it reflected the lies perfectly
What you need's a revolution, I said

The story gave them trouble with their TV reception
So I told it again, starting with their feet
They never touch the ground, I said
Unless you stop riding in cars and walk on unevenness
you'll never see how things look when they're themselves
They laughed and invited me to a party
so I told it again,
I put in it this time the things themselves, exactly as they were
including chimney covers, the numbers of bank accounts

When the story was finished, it was awfully convincing
The people walked into it and picked up the salt shakers
The whole world was in the story,
only I was outside, with a few words
and the revolution.

JAN VAN HEURCK

Islander

Even so, he could not forget the gulls,
Their quiet flight when he had first come there.
He thought of them constantly in old age,
With only breath to write his signature,
Standing on the wrong side of an equals
Sign, watching the mainland from the shore's edge.

Sometimes, he had supposed he should explain
How a face, once loved, was improvised now,
How once he could have played the melody
In any key. But from their eyes, he knew
Their strangeness and playing the years again
Would leave his fingers sore. Though unsteady,

What he had lived was what he had become.
So sensing movement, he looked up for gulls
But found it something to do with the light.
It had always deceived him, like those swirls
Of water flooding his causeway in dream
After dream when in drink and he slept late.

Cultivating his anonymity
Had only pushed the stars further away,
He knew that. But special to the time, burned
A new sun daily on the sea and where
Altered tides spread was where all enmity
Would fail and where gulls had always returned.

IAN CAWS

Stills

FOR MARTIN BENCE

(i)
Entering the dark-room to start work,
you found a thermometer in halves,
under inches of water in the sink.

Its marrow lay as silken, misted
spider's-egg-sac drops of mercury,
essence of monochrome, cinnabar soul.

Already lacking clocks or daylight,
this windowless room had no measure or bounds
from the moment the silver left the glass.

(ii)
An overbrimming pewter bowl of fruit,
bruising with weight, bellying airless below,
where skins purse into lips and colours run.

The house fills with liquor scents that say,
'*Here's proof of patience from trees seen as barren.*'
It's a fragrance from the borders of life and death,

strong and sweet to revive or embalm,
like the smell of spikenard in Lazarus' house,
which lingered for weeks on his sister's hair.

(iii)
Dead things. Flowers like frost aberrations.
Empty seed pods. Scissored scallop shells.
Insects pinned to trays. A rat's skull like a bird's,

the white beak hidden in its nose all along.
It could have been the skull of that moorhen
caught among the rushes in an endless plunge.

You fished it out to take a photograph.
It looked utterly broken, splayed on the bank,
and yet only missing some scintilla.

(iv)
In glass fronted cabinets of static flight,
a kestrel hovers by a hummingbird,
an arctic tern takes a vertical dive.

Pull focus and the bystanders appear
reflected in the glass. Less substantial
than the ranks of the stuffed. It is as though

time among the living has been frozen
to allow the long dead and waiting
to fill their lungs, arch their backs, and wait some more.

(v)
Setting out a still-life on the floorboards,
and light pokes in through the tree outside your window.
Playing resurrection with the objects, with shadows

of the breezing leaves, it's saying '*See that lemon*
spiralling its peel back round itself,
the butterflies and wasps warm waking,

these are all the seeds of animation.'
Then just as quick the light left them for dead,
then back to make the fish swim on its plate.

MICHAEL ROBERTS

The Mary Stanford Disaster

This was the story I tried to tell you in August
and failed, that difficult white week
when the children splashed and swam
in the mouth of the Rother, in the harbour,
and I struggled down too, a lame mermaid,
and overweight, but the only grown woman
to take on the no of the quick strong current,

Who can resist a disaster, said Judy to May,
listen to this, rustling headlines worse day after day.
Voyeur, maggot, parasite, said May to Judy.
This was her special way of calling her mother silly.
But the maggot listens, as the parasite reads:

*A terrible accident struck the small fishing
community of Rye Harbour on the South Coast,
in the morning of November 15, 1928, when*

Mum, there's someone on the phone for you.
I think she said her name was Julia Pope.
She apologised, a stranger long dead, truly scary.
She's talking about these three lads, long dead,
Charlie, Bob and Alec who were three brothers
and my sons were laid out on the beach, stiff, cold,
when the sea delivered them at intervals through the day.

Then I called up to you 'why don't you swim,
it's not so hard, darling, it's lovely'

but you frowned from the quayside,
more than a frown, a private, malevolent
glare. That hard white week in August
in the mouth of the Rother, in Rye Harbour,
when the kids in the river splashed and swam.

Charlie the oldest, my own boy, was floating face down.
Mum, it's a woman crying, a Mrs Pope, PLEASE
He helped me as much as he could in those hard days.
We'd nothing, but there'd always be the fishing.
With two sons without work at home, well, we'd cope.

I didn't know how to explain the horror in August,
that white week. A summer sea mist rose up to hold
the beach in its arms. The old breakwater stumps
stuck up black, an awkward, incomprehensible
mathematical series. A small girl danced and wove
along the black baulks. They were her metronomes,
and then she ran up into the mist.

Bob was my second, silent and broad shouldered.
quiet and observing, his broad face, comfort.
in heavy seas and in the teeth of a howling gale
They ran into the water, caught him as he wavered
half lost in the blinding troughs. And yelled, Alive!
Went the hissed shout. The doctor pumped at him,
but in that uproar my son's quietness departed.

I can't put you down, Julia whoever you are,
you scare me, go out the back door and lock
it behind you. Heavens, I never want to hear
of disasters any more. Caller, you talk
too loud with your howling seas and ill winds.

They say that the last son is the favourite,
his mother's favourite. I don't know. Alec
was a lovely boy, your real spun gold curls
and naughty blue eyes. He had a temper,
he'd kick me on the shins when he was three
and I'd stand him out of the room, then forget
and give him a toffee. 'Thanks ma', he'd say.

Silence fell. Your frown forbade my smile.
You stood by the river, hands on all orifices
as I emerged. Can it be? The sea sucked
at its toffee. It stuck out a hand for our Alec
in heavy seas, in the teeth of a howling gale
He was laid in that cursed lineup, in a giant
roaring like the far howitzers of years before.

May love, switch on the kettle and see that
the door's locked, the wind's getting in its rant.
Don't answer the phone tonight, it's rough out.
Did you know all ghosts are Julia, I had an aunt,
we all had mothers. Sit with me, sweetheart.

Judy, may I call you that, though I'm dead
and you're alive, over a cup of tea, it
was all as real and is all as real as the night
of hell. But it was that morning and the
Mary Stanford rode her useless crab shell
a bit further out, till the giant laid off
and they could wade out and bring her in.

She died in 1929, the very year following;
her daughter said long after, she said,
it was of a broken heart. I walked to the sea

and looked at the old lifeboat house, marooned
and far from anywhere, in the shifting sands.
You turned from my ungainly, naked presence.
'You just can't get it, can you? Don't kid yourself.'

So what's the good? Lovie, tell her to go away.
The mist hangs like a double sheet in my mind,
It flaps slower and slower in the rain each day,
it can't dry like that, dangling heavy and hard
and sodden like a stone from the washing line.

cutting a swathe through families,
in heavy seas, in the teeth of the,
seventeen men out of this hitherto peaceful

All gone and no good to gain for the going.
A wave overturned the lifeboat the Mary Stanford
You forbade all, you forbid all mothers.
Without pause, out of the sky, a mist
came down like a vice on the breakwaters,
children soundlessly darted away, the mothers
clung to the stumps. I heard you howl,

'You fucking bitch, I want to kill you,
I'll never see you again as long as I live.'
There wasn't a wind, nor a wave, but the
arrival of complete silence. I found
her grave. There she lay, the poor woman,
next to her three sons, in the churchyard,
as if stone was a state of shock, permanent.

Mum, it was only a weird thing, you always find
something to worry you, you always worry.

She's rung off. And what if she rings again,
I'll talk to her, there's no hurry, it takes time.
Can't we leave things to mend themselves in the end.

They should have recalled the Mary Stanford,
but they told us that no regulation required it.
(The other ship had been saved.) So she searched
for hours, and then overturned in plain sight of all.
And I, for months, did I rave and scream?
So long ago. Do I talk out of place?
Is it always silence? A vice of silence.

Stone of mist. Does she talk out of place?
This other autumn wind hits fist to hand
off Windover Hill. So long ago.
You forbade all, you forbid everything.
River, river, water, water, remember his face.
In my ears huge waves
roar on wreckage, on error, on wishing.

JUDITH KAZANTZIS

Sweet English Tongue

Hwaet! Beowulf!
I chucked you from a window
the day I took my last exam.
I never thought I'd bless the day I read you,
you and those OE Fragments. I wished then
they'd never found you, mouldering and green
on scraps of rotting parchment, never cleaned
you up and shelved you safe – MS Cott Vit A 15.

I hated having to decipher you –
all those infernal notes I never read –
The blurred adverbial genitives, the runes,
the Old High German datives –
Go and boil your head!

I thought I had got rid of you that day
I flung you from the window
– but you stay.

You stay because the people that lived here
spoke like you, and because the way you speak
lies hidden in my heart. I cannot meet
a word except I ask it if it knows of you.

We used to go to lectures in the Strand
and once a woman in a soft fur coat
said if we'd studied Greek as long as we
had laboured over you, we'd understand

how Homer spoke, Sappho and Aeschylus.
I curse my luck that I had sweated over you
and a few dog-eared Fragments when the true
glory of ancient Greece was lying to my hand.

But now I bless
my little Latin
and less
Greek.
I cannot speak
of wine-dark seas
and rosy-fingered Helens
in my verse.
All those
thick-hyphenated adjectives
that make our bad verse
worse.

I was not born
under an olive
and the high-prowed sun
was not the one
that shone on me.
It was a small flat one.

The men who fought at Maldon
fought for me –
the story of a battle that was lost,
not of the golden gods
who strove and won.

I love my language, and you spoke it, too,
not as I do, but still the thrust is there –

the hard firm consonants, the stride,
the sound of frost and iron
and cold hard air.

When I am sad, it's not the high-prowed ships
of heroes foaming on the salt-lipped sea
that bear me forward on my journeyings,
but with the Wanderer, I
hreran mid hondum hrimcealde sae.

And when I look for comfort, it is not
Aeneas and his band of stranded men
who cheer me up with their philosophy:
'Thaes ofereode, thisses swa maege' speaks.
This is my company.

Just as the fields where they grow sugar beet
can hide the buried urns that hold your dead
under the way I think and write and am
your hard clear words make patterns in my head.

SHEILA UPJOHN

The Reading Hour, 1616

One day he read to me; you look surprised –
Coming from London where you knew him well,
Meeting the daughters, the unlettered wife,
The unconsidered women left behind.
Yes, he was much away, but came in summer,
Grumbled about the garden, talked with friends,
Listened as I went humming round the rooms.
My memory was better for old songs
And for the words of ballads. Long ago,
Crossing the meadow by the winding path
He heard me sing before he saw my face.

I never clung to him, I had the children,
Ruled my own kingdom, happy for a time:
Days without stricture. We would run like truants
Out of the house, the children shrieking joy.
Homeward, they skipped their patterns on the path,
Clutching a posy, wilting honey-stalks
Or drooping crow flowers, their treasure trove.
Yet I was thankful that he was at home
That bitter August when we lost the boy.

You think it strange he should come back at last?
Live as a gentleman? You must remember
This was his town, his country, longer loved
Than friend or mistress; and the man was tired.
The girls are clever, and could talk to him.
But now I felt alone, the odd one out,

And we had missed – for better or for worse –
All the long healing middle span of life.
So, at the end of a back-breaking day,
A Martha with a throbbing head, I found him
Sitting alone; and suddenly the anger
Rose and boiled over, hissing into hate:
He turned, as from a distance – ah, I thought,
How will he treat my silly scalding words –
Though never much to look at, as you know,
There was a steady brightness in his eyes
Hard to resist. He smiled a little: 'Anne,
Come to the fire; let the world slip by;
We're getting old.' And so I slumped, confounded.

Then he began to read: at first the sounds
Tumbled about the room; but here and there
Caught me with laughter: bawdy jokes, and truths,
Colour and noises, of the sand and sea;
Spirits, and young love in a golden time.
Then grief swelled in my throat, for loss, and age,
So this is what he did! and what he knew,
And what he made with words, not dry conceits
But full of earth and moonshine: life itself.

He stopped; his voice had dried; he coughed a bit.
I was tear-blinded, dumb; so there we were,
Stripped of our strangeness, like two shipwrecked souls
Flung naked on a rock, salt in our eyes,
Closer than any time we lay as lovers.

And that was all. Within a day or two
The fever got him. There's no more to tell.
No memorable dying speeches; no
Comets or thunderclaps; a quiet end.

Patches of sunlight shivered on the wall,
A blackbird chattered at the lazy cat.
A common day. His wheel had turned full circle,
April at the beginning and the end.

I sat for a while when the girls had gone,
Testing the silence; would I get used to this?
Once I was easy with the solitude,
Now there were echoes in an empty room.
Resonance of that many-coloured voice
Holding an audience; the reading hour.

Must you be going? and you've come so far
To see and hear so little in this place.
Mind the uneven step – goodnight, my friend.

Dusk in the garden, murmurs from the street.

Sweet of the year in springtime when we sang
Through the green corn, swinging our hands together.

MARCIA NEWBOLT

On a Caspar David Friedrich Painting entitled 'Two Men Observing the Moon'

They have been standing here, tiny hands
clasped behind tiny backs, gazing upwards
at a full moon ever since their arrival 179
years ago. My heart swells with – with what? –
envy, not much but some, also with admiration,
looking at them. So small and so undemanding –
this patch of stony ground has always contented them.
How full their heads are with moon-thoughts!
Though there is more to be said. I for instance
who all my life have been discarding
patches of ground, stony or picturesque makes
no difference, have of late begun gazing upwards
fairly often, more than I used to, I would say,
thinking harmless thoughts. If I had been glimpsed
even one of those times, just then, or then, or
that other time, by someone who walked on past
and never turned to look again,
I'd live in that one mind forever serene as these,
a thought I'll keep, I could say more
but they've shown me there's no need.
How the moon shines! How the two men observe!
And how willingly would I have spent my life
as they have, murmuring small comments
to my friend as the years pass!

DON COLES

Dinners at the Chinese Embassy

A large room, rather shabby
None of the colours matching
And the food served up only slowly, in my memory.
Always for dessert there were lychees
Syrupy, out of tins probably.

To keep the conversation flowing, one of the second
    secretaries
Would occasionally recount the passion of an Emperor for
    his courtesan,
So exquisite she could dance on the outstretched palm of
    his hand.
How he scandalised his mandarins
And sent his eunuchs tittering into the night
When he ordered the horsemen of the imperial mails
    south,
Clattering off on sturdy Mongol ponies
A thousand miles and back to please her with fresh lychees,
Grey as dead flesh within a shale of pink. Dead history is
    safe.

They will never discuss meat cleavers gleaming in the
    London sun
During The Great Proletarian Cultural Revolution,
Though the Ambassador has a nice line, intimate and
    embarrassing,
Of his time in disgrace among the pig farmers.

Nor will we talk of Hong Kong, opium wars, pigtails or
  bound feet smelling of cheese.
Unable ever to relax with foreigners,
As nations, we are too polite to read each others' characters.

STEWART MACNALLY

Bilingual

New weight of language on the tongue;
the tongue tied: intractable, dumb.
The mouth takes shape in a new medium.
Its own breath is less than malleable.
    Speech becomes sculpture:
a six month slow baroque contortion
to form one sentence:

ik stond met m'n mond vol tanden

Sounds freshly unearthed; the mouth
furred, lichen-locked; the tongue's tip curled.
Translation's a technicality: muscular
mastery of the letter R; long division
of the plaintive seagull syllables *ee, ui, ij*:

een enkele reis, alstublieft

The first words are rotund: immaculate,
hard-pressed pebbles on the tongue.
Until the moment of revelation
when they burst like grapes against
the palate, and the tongue, unleashed,
unfurls like a cat and cries: *I am loose
(los). Undone. Just look. I am translated.*

JANE GRIFFITHS

XL

'Mon front est rouge encor du baiser de la reine'

de Nerval

I piss in bottles,
collect cigarette ash in the hollow of my hand,
throw the ends out of the window
or douse them in the sink.

I chew longlife food,
dried fruit, pumpernickel, beef jerky.
I'm forty. I free the jammed light-push with my fingernails
to give the hall a rest.

With one stockinged foot – scrupulous pedantry –
I nudge back the loose stair-carpet on the eleventh step.
Later I might slam some doors
and spend a wet evening under a tree.

I've identified with a yellowish fox beside the railway line,
followed silent firework displays on the Thames,
seen two shooting stars burn out over London
and made wishes on them.

I can't remember when I last wrote a letter
or picked up the telephone. My smile
goes on shopkeepers and bus drivers and young mothers.
It dazzles me.

I think continually about money, and the moths eat my
    clothes:
the thing about earthly treasures was true.
For half an hour, amid palpitations, I watched
two children I was sure were mine.

Most of the day I'm either lying down
or asleep. I haven't read this many books
this avidly since I was a boy.
Nights are difficult. Sometimes I shout.

I'm quarrelsome, charming, lustful, inconsolable, broken.
I have the radio on as much as ever my father did,
carrying it with me from room to room.
I like its level talk.

MICHAEL HOFMANN

Suicide Bridge

There must be a suicide bridge in every city.
Ours is high and thin and old.
Its angular legs remind me of some frail spider,
Poised to play the piano, or collapse or run.
We have earthquakes here. I don't like to cross it.
It's never checked, there are cracks and rust, missing bolts.
But there's nothing to fear on such a glorious day.

A beautiful day, all brightness and smells of dryness.
Months of mud and rain, suddenly over.
Still, with no wind to carry high the odour
of tin ghetto and river, and pampas grass
writhing below the high slung road.
What a fall from grace for whoever decided
that there was nothing to fear on such a glorious day.

People were compelled to stop and make faces.
Squinting into the abyss. The bridge tilting,
pulled by a dead hand, and tilting
under the unusual stress, of the crying cyclist
who was just passing and called out.
Did this sunless diver pause, before the other leg
was swung over, with nothing to fear on such a glorious day.

MARIANNE VIZINCZEY-LAMBERT

The Shapes of Things

A circle
for his mother's face;
circles for apples, oranges, the sun.

Squares and triangles
with his birthday crayons
for their tiny house;
a wavy line
for the chimney-smoke.

It was always the shapes of things.

What a gift
with nothing but brushes and paint
to find the shape of a hawk circling,
a duststorm,
a woman's head turning.

Nobody understood
how he could fit them
into such a small space:
the shape of loving,
the shapes of hurt and comfort,
joy and despair.

He learnt
the shape of fast cornering,
of seduction,

of smart parties in the best circles,
of power and respect.
He found out
the special shape of money.

Do you know
the shape of illness,
of unpaid bills,
of friends who let you down?
The shape of loss?
Look at his self-portraits.

Look at those eyes
that learnt the shape of the whole world.

On the last day of his life
leaning on a stick
trembling in front of the easel
he drew a perfect circle.

MICHAEL SWAN

The Bracelet

Fanned out, lark-risers, men and boys fishing
along the parapet of a long low bridge,
all morning landing this and that, when one son
sniggles something furious on the riverbed,
a deep feeder, heavy, a live wire raging against
its torrential luck (for it's a secular fish),
the boy reeling back, rapidly freezing,
dragging its weight in slow motion then giving slack,
then letting go, allowing the fierce catch
to drive forward thinking itself free (an idealistic fish),
only for him to reel and haul and let go again
his ankles braced with the pressure
into the angle of the wall, if once
then a dozen times, until the evil streak of liquid,
that slippery apodal anger, snaps clear,
is spat out by the fast shallow river
and its stonewashed Ophelias, and ascends writhing,
tying and untying itself like the bait on the barbs
clutching its slimy guts. Fearless,
the boy wrestles the shining hatred to the ground
to remove the immovable hook, making
the wild thing curl, squeeze and embrace
like a long-lost forearm his forearm, from genuine pain
or overt affection, in a lithe Celtic pattern,
a *fin-de-siècle* spiral, an ornate looping bracelet
that would stay with the youngster, the scar
from knuckles to elbow ready to spring to life
when he eats that flayed devil boiled with onions,
its vicious alien head imprinted on his palm.

HOWARD WRIGHT

The Tightrope Wedding

We can't take our eyes off the young
couple walking to meet one another
on this cable strung between twin
towers of the castle. Fifty feet

up in the air and no net. Arms
wide, they're holding out matching
aluminium balancing poles
that are light but so long they bow slightly.

We can see how the slim, dark-haired
and suited groom bends his knees
as he leans forward shifting his weight
onto the front foot to take

his next step. The bride, we assume,
must be doing the same, somehow
holding sway over her stiff
petticoats, the satin and lace;

and, adjusting to any gust
tugging at her train, she comes on
steadily, one white shoe showing,
its soft sole curved over the rope.

They're wired up, they counterbalance
each other, but they're not one flesh yet.
We bite our lips, can't bear to look,
are grateful to be distracted

by this tubby, game, down-to-earth priest
about to climb into the picture
up the fire appliance's steep
but not impossible ladder.

MICHAEL LASKEY

An Angry Heart,
An Empty House

AN AISLING –

Aisling: 'Political vision poems of the 18th century in
which the beautiful princess *Eire* bewails her lot and awaits
redress through a Stuart prince' (Professor P.L. Henry in
'Poems of Irish Women', The Mercier Press, 1990). The
form has been used most recently by Thomas Kinsella in
'Butcher's Dozen'.

Tonight as anger filled my heart
I thought the house was empty too.
But then a vision made me start,
It was a woman, one I knew.
She had no need to ring the bell,
All human doors are air to her,
For as the Gaelic poets tell,
Her being knows no barrier.
She was a woman made from sky,
As blue as perfect mornings are,
And yet a tear stood in her eye,
A darkness-needing evening star.

But when she spoke to me her tone
Was down-to-earth and blunt. 'This way
Of writing is,' she said, 'fly-blown
And mouldy now. But that's OK
With me, provided who I am

Is first made clear. Come on, come clean,
Admit this vision is a sham,
I'm just a cursor on a screen,
A pixelled dot, a flightless dart.
There is no magic woman here,
No other-worldly Irish art,
No star, no visionary tear.
But if you must pretend, discard
The lukewarm certainties of doubt.
You're sick with rage, so swallow hard,
Then cough it up and spit it out.'

That's just the thing I want to do,
I said, but words come hard to me.
The chaos we've been living through
This quarter of a century –
The Northern thing that makes us turn
The TV off or skip the page,
Or if it doesn't makes us burn
With horror at the facts and rage
Against the news – has struck me dumb.
My anger goads me on, but when
I try to speak the words won't come,
They choke for lack of oxygen.
And even if I could presume
To write, the stink of so much death –
Three thousand bodies in one tomb –
Would stifle any poet's breath.

'The more there is of death the less
It means,' she said. 'The thing to do
Is concentrate and then compress
All of your Christs into one Jew –

A single crucifixion will
Suffice to represent the rest.'

That is, I said, impossible,
For Irish folk are unimpressed
By God himself if he's just One
And not – excuse the blasphemy –
A Ghost whose Father is His Son.
For us the truth is trinity,
So that is why I've tried to pick
Three crimes to carry all this weight –
One Protestant, one Catholic,
One British, somewhat less than Great . . .

Where I begin is history now;
Another poet's raised his voice
To tell in 'Butcher's Dozen' how
In Derry 14 men and boys
Were shot to death, a savagery
Made worse when it was justified
As legal by Lord Widgery.
The soldiers took the oath and lied;
They told the judge they only fired
When someone shot at them, that those
They killed were armed. It then transpired
The nail-bombs hidden in their clothes
Had – abracadabra! – disappeared
Into thin air. His lordship said
(And even hardened newsmen sneered)
He blamed the murdered for being dead –
What else could rioters expect?
The poet's maddened phantom screams:

'England, the way to your respect
Is via murderous force, it seems.'[1]

Such threatenings were common then,
But Kinsella, who chose the case
With care, was struck by silence when
'It seems' became a commonplace.
He wrote what others felt and might
Have been expected to rejoice
That history had proved him right,
But, faced with murder, lost his voice.

'This noble silence I suppose,'
She said, 'you shared?' I felt her eyes
Bore into mine and thought of those
This poem will try to satirize
And couldn't speak, for I'd been loud
In my own way: the fantasy
That marched a huge and stupid crowd
Upon the British Embassy
Was one that I had shared, alas.
I'd cheered the man who'd climbed up to
A first floor window, smashed the glass,
And then out of his pocket drew
A petrol-bomb. The bottle had a twist
Of rag for wick, but here's the catch,
Our patriotic arsonist
Forgot to bring a bloody match.
But someone threw a box and then

[1] From 'Butcher's Dozen' by Thomas Kinsella, published by the Peppercanister Press, 1972. Quoted by permission from the author.

The air was filled with sulphur for
This angel who, now proud again,
Could fall to work, like Lucifer.
Our anger, though, was not to be
Extinguished by a blaze. As good
As burning was, the thirst that we
Desired to slake cried out for blood.
A diplomatic incident was not
Enough to satisfy that need:
The Christian thing to do was what
They did to us: to make them bleed.

We didn't have too long to wait.
Within a month we gave the Brits
The chance to show what made them Great:
The guts that brought them through the Blitz.
I happened at the time to make
My living as a journalist.[2]
The day this news began to break
Our Foreign Sub banged down his fist
And roared: The Paratroops have got
Their answer now! A bomb has been
Put under them in Aldershot!
The roof's come down on their canteen!
The newsroom rang with howls of joy.
They'd murdered us. We'd murdered them.
And I joined in, a roaring boy
Who cheered the butchers' requiem.

[2] As a sub-editor in the Evening Press, part of the Irish Press group
founded by Eamon de Valera. For a description of the internal rebellion
against the Irish Press editorial line on the North see the history of the
newspaper, *More Kicks Than Pence*, by Michael O'Toole, published by
Poolbeg Press, 1992.

At first the body-count was ten,
Three less than Bloody Sunday, though
That evened out a little when
The news came through a Holy Joe,
A padre, had been shown the way
To heaven. He can count as three,
Some joker quipped — I have to say
I laughed, like hell. But when the smoke
Had cleared at last and all the dead
Had been identified the joke
Was even funnier. Instead
Of threshing Paratroops to chaff
They'd mowed the man who cut the grass
And — oopsadaisy, what a laugh! —
Five members of the female class,
Five women scrubbers, wielding mops
Instead of guns, who soaped the floors
And slopped about in old flip-flops
And scarves and nylon overalls.
Charladies charred and barbecued!
If only they'd been men, with balls,
Their corpses would have looked less rude.
But women, well, that was a bit
Of an embarrassment of course,
Though, not to put a tooth in it,
They shouldn't have been there, the whores,
For as a woman living in
A brothel is a prostitute
A scrubber who is skivvying
For Paras wears a parachute.

But that was not the kind of stuff
One said in public. There, along

With anger, grief and other guff,
One found 'the underlying wrong'.
This was, one hardly had to say,
A crime, by any definition,
But would we have the IRA
Without the evils of Partition?
Our islands shared the same distress,
And yet the cause of this disorder,
According to the Irish Press,
Was not the bombers but the border.
Besides, this sad atrocity,
Which horrifies us all, no doubt,
Will get far more publicity,
Our leader writer pointed out,
Than Derry did a month ago.

The man who called this kettle black
Was not himself as white as snow.
Our nickname for the steaming hack
Was suitable enough: Tin Pot,
For Tim Pat Coogan had, God knows,
A canny way with words (if not,
Alas, with grammar or with prose).
Like Popeye scoffing spinach, tin
And all, he'd swallow with a gulp
Whatever was Republican
And vomit up its greenish pulp
Or fart it out in clouds of gas.
Well, even now he makes me think
And stop. For who am I to pass
Such judgements on another's stink?
I ought to sniff at self instead:
I hadn't murdered, yet the guilt

Was in my heart and on my head
Was blood that I had never spilt.
I'd thought that hatred was absurd,
A god designed by atheists,
And yet I too prayed with the herd,
Their tribal anger clenched my fists.

The woman spoke, her eyes ablaze
Her scornful tears: 'It is a curse
To think confession can erase
Your guilt because it's made in verse.
You're wrong. Polluted at its source,
Your poem will be a non-event
Unless it speaks with pure remorse
And not this self-advertisement.

'I'll tell myself your second tale,
It is the story of a young
And voiceless girl, a nightingale
Who died because she lost her tongue.'

But then she stopped. A dreadful fright
Took hold of me. Oh speak, I cried. . . .

'My heart is full of Margaret Wright,'
She said at last, 'and how she died.
There are some things so alien
To light it's best to turn away
From seeing them, and this is one.
It's dark. I've got nothing to say.
And so I must. I'll sing for her
The song of cemetery birds
And as I do, her mouth, that blur
Of worms, I'll cleanse with eerie words.'

And now another, smaller, voice came out.
The accent was a Belfast girl's, the kind
That once upon a time perhaps had sung
That Albert Mooney said he loved her, all
The boys were thinking of her. Out it came
As white as snow, but infinitely sad
And cold, as hollow as the rings she wore
Upon her finger bones, more mournful than
The little bells that tinkled on her toes.
Old Johnny Murray said she'd die
If she didn't get the fella
With the roving eye.[3]
She'd got her wish.
A man had fixed his gaze on her
And she had died.

This ghost now spoke. She said:

'My name is Wright but I was wrong:
I didn't fit, I couldn't work
At any kind of job for long
Before my brain began to jerk
And fizzle in my puzzled skull.
It played with me, like cat and mouse,
As if I was invisible,
A spirit in an empty house.
Those epileptic spasms split
My life in two: my home was good,

[3] Adapted from the Belfast street song which begins, 'I'll tell me ma,
when I get home,/The boys won't leave the girls alone'. It also includes the
lines, 'Albert Mooney says he loves her,/All the boys are thinking of her',
and 'Knock on the door, ring on the bell,/O my true love, are you well?/
Out she comes as white as snow,/Rings on her fingers,/Bells on her toes'.

I was my mother's favourite,
A window in her widowhood.
And we believed. I was a Prod
And proud of it; my room, kept clean
And neat, displayed my faith in God:
Beside a photo of the Queen
I'd framed a picture of a lamb
Embroidered on a linen sheet
And round its head I'd stitched the Psalm:
Thy word's a lamp unto my feet.
I was, I hoped, a child of light.
And yet I also knew the dark.
There was another Margaret Wright,
A woman driven by a spark
Within her head to run away,
Get on a bus downtown and then
Go wandering, get lost all day
And in the night be found by men.
You know their sort? No matter that
I hardly knew my name or where
I was, there'd always be some cat
Who liked a mouse and didn't care
If it was too far gone to play
The game of sex, that little death
In which the self, a willing prey,
Allows the cat to catch its breath.
But even in their claws, the eye
That looked at them was cold, a glare
That drove them off; the only sigh
They heard a sob of pure despair,
The kind a prisoner makes at last
When he accepts the only way
To force his present be the past

Demands he throw the key away,
To tunnel in instead of out,
Draw over him a crushing quilt
Of stone, and from its dumbness shout
'My only innocence is guilt. . . .'

And yet I could break through that chain.
Somehow, some day, some night, I'd wake
And find myself at home again
And feel once more, once more, the ache
Of being in my mother's arms,
Forgiven for the hurt that I
Had done us both – her love still warms
The grave wherein my bones now lie.

But then, one final time, the fuel,
That petrol electricity,
Ignited in my brain its cruel
Need to burn and, burning, flee.
I fled. I didn't say goodbye.
For me the house was empty too,
Get out! Get out! its frantic cry.
So, like a moth on fire, I flew
Into the night. The streets, ablaze
With haloed lamps, were dark to me.
How long I baffled through this maze,
The Long Kesh of our geography –
That block is theirs, this one is mine –
Or once it was – I cannot say.
But all the same I knew the line
I had to take, the safest way
To go from south to north Belfast.
The Village there, the place in which

Somehow I ended up at last
That April night, is only rich
In Protestants, a people poor
But generous to strangers when
They feel their hearts, like mine, are pure.
The only thing I can condemn,
Their plate-glass silence, soon was cracked –
I'll tell that story bye and bye:
It's still the only violent act
My broken heart is mended by. . . .'

She stopped. That woman of the air who had
Been speaking for this woman of the earth
Could not go on. I knew the reason why:
The time had come for Margaret to tell
The story of her death and even she,
Who'd opened up this tomb and rolled its stone
Aside, as poetry is meant to do,
Had reached the lightness limit of her art.
At last she gathered up her strength and from
Her mouth the smaller voice came out again,
But slower now, the sounds it made as dark
And heavy as a flock of graveyard crows.

'The place I'm in is painted black.
It's windowless, a blank concrete
Flat-roofed shed off a cul-de-sac
Down at the end of Meridi Street.
A flute-band is supposed to use
The hall for practising. In fact
It's just a shebeen where cheap booze
And dope are sold. And now it's packed . . .

'I'd knocked. Behind the chipboard door
I heard the bolts being drawn.
They opened on a muffled roar.
A tattooed bouncer loomed: Come on,
He said, come in. And in I went,
As white and silently as snow.
The smoky air inside was rent
By flashing lights. The vertigo
I felt and all my drunkenness
Had deafened me. I didn't hear
The roaring voices fade or guess
That I had changed the atmosphere.

'At first they only circled round,
Like nervous partners at a dance
For debutantes, but I just frowned
And stared like something in a trance,
A creature hypnotized by light,
A mouse that doesn't run away
But waits, unconscious of its fright,
Until the cat comes out to play.
A little tap, a tiny nudge
From one big paw I felt at first
Upon my arm. I didn't budge.
A face came close to mine and cursed
With stinking breath into my ear:
I said, it said, what is your name
And what the fuck are you doing here?
For who I was and how I came
To be in hell I had no word.
Perhaps I said, I'm feeling sick
And said it so he thought he heard
Me say, I am a Catholic.

I must have made that sort of slip.
Why else would he have screamed so loud:
We've got a Popehead in the kip!
A Popehead? Me, who was so proud
Of being a Prod! They prodded me
At first, the way a Judas goat
Is goaded till the pack can see
The way is open to its throat.
And like hyenas too, the craft
Of teasing me to death was fun:
They howled with joy and as they laughed
They gathered in a ring and spun
Me like a parcel in a game.

'The females of the species too
Were keen to prove they were the same
As men, or better, since they knew
The way a woman's pride is hurt:
One held my hands, as if to dance,
Another lifted up my skirt
And stripped me of my tights and pants.
Oh Jesus, in your final loss
You weren't as cruelly mocked as me.
You weren't as naked on the cross
As Margaret Wright was forced to be.
It was my sex that drove them wild,
And so I'm glad for memory's sake
To say I never had a child.
How could I bear the endless ache
Of being here if I had borne
A son or daughter on the earth
Who'd have to think of me and mourn
The day that I had given birth?

'It seemed as first that mocking me
Was game enough. But when I thought
They'd seen it all the mockery
Got uglier. One joker caught
My hair and then another one
Began to slap me on the head.
But when I lay there, still as dumb
As snow, they hit me till I bled
With fists and billiard cues, the shaft
They'd broken off a sweeping brush
And other clubs. And still they laughed!
How comical it was, the gush
Of blood that spurted from my nose.
How funny too the way I crept
Across the floor without my clothes.
They laughed so much they almost wept.

'But then, as if they'd hit a wall,
They stopped. The screeching music too
Cut out. Across the crowded hall
A rippling wave of silence flew
As fast as light but heavier.
They held their breath. I never thought
That air could be so weighty or
So still. A glint of steel had caught
Their eyes, a gleam of something black.
Just as I saw it was a gun
They bagged me with a plastic sack.
I knelt there like a naked nun
And tried to pray. But no words came.
How could I beg for mercy when
I didn't even know my name?

'The crowd began to breathe again
But now they didn't laugh. Instead,
Like beasts who've scented blood, they sighed.
I felt the gun against my head.
For Christ's sake, Ian, someone cried,
Let's get the fucker out of here.
The store room's safe. We'll do it there.
I tried to rise but, weak with fear,
I fell again. They grabbed my hair
And dragged me out across the floor
Into another smaller room.
I heard a click – they'd locked the door.
And then they hit me with the broom
And with the billiard cue again,
And with each blow they asked me who
I thought I was. I was insane
With fright and suffocating too
Inside the sack. I couldn't speak,
I couldn't tell them anything. . . .'

And then? And then? And then?

'And then
I felt the gun against my cheek,
But didn't hear the deafening
Explosion that the bullet made.
Four times they fired. Four waves of light
Mixed up with blood and smoke were sprayed
Against the wall and Margaret Wright
Was dead. I died as silently
As any woman ever did.

'But that was not the end for me.

My killers still had to get rid
Of what was left, the rubbish in
The tattered sack, the bloody slush
Of bone and brain. A wheelie bin
Was what they used. They had to crush
Me into it. What could they do?
They couldn't get the lid to shut
Because one leg stuck up. They threw
A coat across its dirty foot,
Unlocked the door and wheeled me out.
The hall was empty now – a cloud
Of cigarette smoke whirled about
The lights to show how fast the crowd
Had fled the bullets' leaden roar.
Among the broken glass the clothes
I'd worn were scattered on the floor.
The only sound, the stereo's
Electric hum, droned on and on.

'My killers ran me down the road
Until at last they came upon
A terraced house. A streetlamp showed
Its eyes were blind. Someone had bricked
The windows up against the rain.
The place was vacant, derelict.
Beside it was a high-walled lane,
A narrow passageway, unlit.
They dragged the bin down there into
The dark and tipped me out of it.
One climbed the wall. The other two
Took hold and swung me to the top.
But I was slippery with blood.
They lost their grip and let me drop.

A nail snagged off the plastic hood
And then they saw that Margaret Wright
Was looking up at them. At first
They were so overcome by fright
They froze, but then with one last burst
Of panic and of rage they hauled
And shoved and pulled me up the wall.
There for a moment I lay sprawled
And then the catcher let me fall
Into the stinking yard below.

'The place was full of things like me,
Soft stuff in bags, a sodden dough
Of food and clothes but cushiony
To land in, if it hadn't been
Mixed up with splintered furniture,
The steely guts of some machine
And other bits of junk which were
So broken and so old they'd gone
Beyond the need for names, like me.

'But when the sun came up and shone
Into the yard it saw that we
Had settled down and made the most
Of turning rigid in the frost.
I was at one with them, a ghost
Who'd found a home by being lost
Among the homeless. Out of sight,
And out of mind, impervious
To cold, we waited till the night
Once more drew darkness over us.
Foot loose and fancy free and far
Removed from any worldly powers,

We waited for the morning star
And fused its innocence with ours.

'So, peacefully, the sky turned grey,
But then a stranger climbed the wall
And saw my face. I heard him say
Oh Jesus! Jesus Christ!, then call
For help – that name and cry belong
Together but their pleadings, meek
As they are, can't prevent the strong
From coming late and being weak.
But, still, they came. Nor did they laugh.
Policemen and detectives sighed
While someone took my photograph
From every angle like a bride
Who's just been married, blushing pink
With happiness – it was so rude
The way I stared and didn't blink
An eye although I was quite nude.
Well, that was that. Another day
Was done. Their gloves and plastic smocks
Were taken off. They drove away
In cars. I followed in a box. . . .'

'You know the rest,' the spirit said.
'A man called Ian Hamilton
Was kidnapped, tortured and shot dead.
He was, his killers claimed, the one
Responsible for what occurred,
But since they too were UVF
Or Red Hand Gang, the claim's absurd,
The hearsay story of a deaf
And dumb witness. Another man,

Called Stephen Rules, has also been
Accused, but he's more lucky than
His friend, for justice will be seen
And done to him, with innocence
Presumed, and even if his guilt
Is proved he will not recompense
With his own blood the blood he spilt.
No plucking out of eye or tooth
Will pay his debt. And yet his tongue,
Uncut, in time will speak this truth:
Remorse, is worse than being hanged.'[4]

The smaller voice now spoke again.
It tone was calm, as if the void
The bullets opened in her brain
Had filled with kindness, unalloyed
With leaden hatred, for the man
Who'd died for her.

'For me,' she said,
'There is no greater anguish than
To know that someone else has bled
To staunch my wound. My darkest hour
Is neither lightened nor reversed
By spilling blood. Revenge is sour,

[4] Stephen Rules is serving a life sentence for the murder, as is
Christopher Sheals. Others convicted of offences associated with the
crime are: David Jess, seven years for assisting offenders and five years
for membership of a proscribed organisation (the Red Hand
Commando); Warren Gibson, seven years for assisting offenders and five
years for membership of the Red Hand Commando; Stephen Salters,
seventeen years for assisting offenders; and Alison Elliott, three years for
assisting offenders.

Not sweet to me. And yet my thirst
For retribution was assuaged
By one communal violent act:
The people on that street, enraged
By what had happened there, attacked
The pit where no one pitied me.
As fierce for good as were the fiends
For foul, they got a JCB
And smashed the place to smithereens.
The shambles of my death was not
To be commemorated by
A slaughter house. To mark the spot
Where drunken butchers bled me dry
There's nothing, just a vacancy.
There is no other monument
I need, except your memory
Of who I was: a woman sent
Into the world to learn the most
There is to know of guilt and shame
And then, for you, become a ghost
Who wanders searching for her name.

'I feel my voice is failing now.
The grave I'm in is dark and deep
And yet it's kindly too. Allow
My spirit rest in peace and sleep.
O let me sleep, just let me sleep. . . .'

Long hours of silence slowly passed.
But then the spirit spoke at last.
'There is', she said, 'a final tale to tell.
A louder story from a deeper hell.'

We've heard, I said, the story of a death
So cruel that it took away your breath.
How could there be another sound as loud
As Margaret's silence in her plastic shroud?

'Her fate,' she said, 'however hideous,
Was not designed to frighten all of us.
Poor Margaret lost her life by accident
And those who murdered her were ignorant,
A drunken lumpenproletariat
Who killed a woman for the sake of it.
What Jesus said, though hard, must still be true:
Forgive them, Lord, they know not what they do.
But murder planned and plotted in cold blood
Entwines itself with wickedness for good.
Yet even this is understandable
When those who die are linked to those who kill.
To murder, though, a man you've never known
Is in a class of evil on its own.
The story you are going to tell belongs
Among that category of human wrongs
The fearful memory of which will last
Until the time for memory is past.'

I spoke:

The known facts are these – they're very few –
There was a Derryman, aged forty-two,
Whose name was Pat; he had a wife, Kathleen,
And children; in the papers I have seen
Their numbers given, three, but otherwise
We have to guess if they are girls or boys.
The family name, Gillespie, is more terse

Than our *Mac Giolla Easbuig* is in Erse.
It's short for Bishop's Servant's Son, and that,
Peculiarly enough, describes our Pat:
He was, in fact, a chef, although his feasts,
It must be said, were not consumed by priests.
The men he served, served not the Nazarene,
Instead they took their orders from the Queen.
And this, of course, annoyed the IRA –
To brew up tea for troops is not a way
An Irishman should earn a living wage.
To save himself a stuffing, he'd be sage,
They said, to quit the kitchen – save your soul
For your *bonne femme* by living on the dole
Their recipe. But Patsy was a fool
And stubborn too. He let his feelings rule
The way he lived – for instance in his craze
For giving to his kids what nowadays
Is called a better quality of life.
And what is even crazier, his wife
Supported him. That could only mean
She too was part of Britain's war machine,
A soldier in a skirt, an English Rose,
Diana-like, in Marks and Spencer clothes,
Who wore a Union Jack beneath her clothes

They warned the bitch,
But she and Patsy felt that this was rich,
Coming as it did from those who thought
A job was only good if you weren't caught
While doing it – such bourgeois snobbery
About a little light armed robbery!

But all the same just shooting Patsy down
Would hardly do much damage to the Crown,
Although, some thought, one dead Gillespie might
Suffice to teach the gift of second sight
To other minor Catholic bureaucrats
Who didn't know they were as blind as bats.
There were some others, though, who felt that this
Could harm relations with the populace.
It might, they said, not serve the cause
Of good PR, like shooting Santa Claus.
OK to blast a soldier or a cop
But if they shot a cook, well, could they stop
At that? And if they didn't weren't there
Too many of such traitors everywhere?
Builders who supplied the Brits with stuff?
To nut the likes of them was fair enough.
But what about a census-taker who,
As it happened, was a woman too?
Afraid of being sexist – oh, for dread! –
They let her have a bullet in the head.[5]
But killing Pat, that worthless little cur,
Couldn't they do something witter?
They could, they could indeed: to add insult
To injury they'd make a catapult
And let him, sinless, be the stone it cast.
They'd put him on a bomb and let him blast
The army barracks at Fort George to hell!
(Besides, it wouldn't waste *matériel*.)

[5] On 7 March 1981 Carol Mather, aged twenty-six, was shot dead in
Derry while collecting census forms.

But sad to say, the first time that they tried,
In '86, they got the van inside
The gates all right, but Pat jumped out, the gom,
And in a tick the Brits defused the bomb.
Of course, this was, like time, a passing thing
And yet the IRA could hardly bring
Themselves to think of screwing up again.
Indeed, the planning of the next campaign
Was lengthy – all of four long years. But still,
You'll understand, there were more graves to fill
Than Pat Gillespie's one – so many more
In fact, to count them all would be a bore.
But think they did. And what they thought was nice.
In 1990 – or to be precise
About the Fall, October 23rd –
Kathleen was going to bed but when she heard
The phone she answered it. 'Is Patsy in?'
'He is of course.' (Where else would he have been?)
'I think it's time for him to be in bed,'
The voice replied and then the line went dead.
At once there came a knock upon the door.
Pat should not have opened it before
Inquiring who it was. And yet he did.
The fact that woollen balaclavas hid
Their faces quickly gave the game away –
Our wolves are sheepish beasts on judgement day.
They flocked into the house. It seemed too small
For such a crowd, what with their guns and all.
Telling Kathleen not to worry, that,
If he was good, no harm would come to Pat,
And he'd be back in only half an hour,
They led him out. Don't ask did they allow her
Give him a final kiss – it's such bad taste

To be so sentimental, such a waste
Of time when all the reader wants to know
Is how the story goes. But even so
It's worth considering a little what
The likely consequences of a lot
Of kissing would have been, for if the boys
Allowed a last embrace, who knows the noise
She might have made. She'd more than probably
Have thrown a wobbler, gone all slobbery.
So all in all it was considerate
That kissing Patsy was prohibited,
Unthinkable indeed, in all respects,
Like letting Siamese twins engage in sex.

So Kathleen saw the double of her heart
Being led away. Their vow – till death us part –
She didn't understand was then being kept,
But all the same she sensed it and she wept
As widows do. The car drove off – to where
No one will ever say who wasn't there;
All we know is that it must have been
Secure enough to use without being seen –
The engineers had lots of work to do
Before the night was out. Time flew
For them, but back in Patsy's house it slowed
So much the kitchen clock seemed to explode
The silence with its tiny thunderous boom.
Between each click a stillness filled the room,
Each second longer than a century.

The guards relaxed. Did Kathleen make them tea
To while the years away? It was the kind
Of thing she would have done. And did they mind

Being seen the while their hoods were lifted up
To sip the non-inebriating cup?
And did they talk the usual sort of blether:
Folks they knew, the telly and the weather?
Or politics? The Anglo-Irish Pact?
Well, not the first, for Volunteers who yacked
About the sort of people that they met
Got warnings they weren't likely to forget:
A fitting for a wooden overcoat.
And politics? Discussing how to vote
Might seem a little futile to a wife
Whose husband is about to lose his life –
They held that though we all deserve to live
That principle is, well, just relative.
Exceptions – her relation – proved the rule.
Explaining that would make you look a fool,
So politics was barred and gossip too
Was out of bounds. What else was there to do
To pass the time away?

You'll understand,
Of course, I'm going on with this goddamned
Recital for a reason. Four of them
In fact. Four hours from bloody Bethlehem
These beasts were slouching in while drinking tea.
This is a bore, but boredom's poetry
In motion when its opposite is prose,
A sentence ending where God only knows.

Four hours – a fraction of the time unknown
To history – went by, and then the phone
Began to ring. Three times, like Peter's cock,
It crowed, and then – an even greater shock –

It stopped. That's it, we've had our fun,
The leader said to Kate. Pat's job is done,
He'll soon be home. But that was not the truth.
He knew, as did the watcher in the booth,
Putting down the phone, whatever Pat
Was doing he would not be doing that.

And why? I'll tell you why – to stop him from
Escaping they had strapped him to the bomb,
They'd bound him to the driver's seat so fast
He couldn't free himself before the blast,
And if for any reason he should try
Then Kathleen and his kids instead would die.
Did Patsy know? He did. He knew full well
He'd got a roasted snowball's chance in hell
Of getting out. But still he tried to drive
As if by driving he would not arrive,
And by obeying not obey the laws
Of logic, play Herod as a Santa Claus
Who cuts his throat and thinks the blood that flows
Is not his own, although he also knows
The baby's crying sounds familiar,
The gurgling usual, but sillier.
Thus suicidal Pat, a man grenade,
Went hurtling towards the soldiers' barricade.

(They only get a mention – there's no sense
In wasting time on their experience
Of being what they weren't: part of the whole
Who send to know for whom the bell will toll.
Besides, they're shown to be inferior
By no one now remembering who they were,
Except their relatives – like Pat indeed,

Forgotten in the time it takes to read
These slowed down lines.)

Look back. He's there. Look here.
He's driving towards the checkpoint, drawing near
Enough to let the sentry see his face.
For all we know it may have been the case
That Patsy and the soldier recognised
Each other from the mess-hall, realised,
Perhaps, they'd talked about their families once
Upon a time. I wonder what he wants
At this unearthly hour, the soldier may
Have thought.

(Excuse me, please, this long delay
In getting to the point – it's just a trick,
An old technique to let these moments prick
Their pins in you and slowly perforate
Your brain. Long ages pass. They're worth their weight
In gold and silver to a simple poet,
For poetry is time before you know it.)

You stop to think . . . And as you do you feel
That someone's watching you with eyes of steel.
You're wrong. It isn't you this bird of prey
Is looking at. It's Patsy on his way
Up to the checkpoint.

Check the timer. Wait.
Now flick the switch. The circuits integrate.
The pulse – so slowly – leaps across the road.
Makes contact.

Patsy and the van explode.

Its metal and his flesh are harmonised
And married in a flash. By joy surprised,
Their atoms intermingle in a mist
Of rising rain. Oh, love's their catalyst!
It was a miracle much greater than
The one performed by Christ. That Son of Man
Was only able to turn bread and wine
To flesh and blood. Now, that's all very fine
Perhaps, but is it quite as big a deal
As turning Pat into a steering wheel?
Transforming human nature was God's plan
But here was something new: a Transit Man!
It was a most extraordinary marriage,
To couple Cain and Cana in a carriage.
How wonderful it was: to take a bloke and mate
Him with a truck! To transubstantiate
A Bishop's Servant to a vehicle,
Now that is what I'd call a miracle.
What God has kept apart, dear brethren, may
Be joined together by the IRA.

Five soldiers and the checkpoint disappear,
As if they were the snows of yesteryear.
The injured – thirty local dreamers dreaming
Who woke to hear there's more than sirens screaming –
Are rushed to hospital. A fire consumes
Some twenty houses, and where once were rooms
The stinks of gas and ruptured drains compete
Against the scent of roasted human meat.

The sun comes up, the highest dust falls down,
Uniting Patsy with his native town.

The bombers, breakfasting on eggs and rashers,
Are thinking, This'll frizzle Maggie Thatcher's
Appetite, but let her scoff this smidgen:
All's fair in love and war and in the kitchen.

Now, after breakfast and a little rest –
The kids at school, the awe-struck wife caressed –
The time has come to go and be debriefed
By one they say – if they can be believed –
Is Chief of Staff, the top Provisional.
A man whose eyes reflect an iron will,
The mirror to a mouth so tightly zipped
It looks as if a cut-throat razor slipped
And made a slit whose smile is like a ruin
Illuminated by a sickle moon.

I stopped. The man deserves to be in jail,
I said, but isn't this beyond the pale?
I wonder is it fair to introduce
Into my poem mere personal abuse.

'Well, names will never hurt a man whose soul
Is nourished by a human casserole.
Besides, the men who'd served him up this choice
Repast adored, like dogs, their master's voice.
Attentively they listened while he praised
The way that Pat Gillespie had been braised.'

Who is this Cook of Cooks, this Chef of Stiffs?

'McGuinness is his name. He contradicts,
It must be said, the many writers who
Assert he is the Master of the Barbecue.
That is, he says, a dirty tricks campaign,
An orchestrated libel on Sinn Fein,
The party which he's proud to represent
And which elected him Vice-President . . .'

I interrupted her. So far, I said,
The only people that I've named are dead,
Or if they aren't, like Tim Pat, they're free
To go to court and sue the pants off me.
Why should you now add to the body count
A living man and call him to account
For crimes you only think he may have done?
Are you so sure he is the guilty one?
Besides, a year ago the IRA
Decided death should have a holiday.
What point is there in making such a fuss
Now that McGuinness is being good for us?

'To him,' she said, 'your goodness is a myth,
And excrement is what he rhymes it with.
For him this is an interlude, a lull
In which he'll use the peace to goad John Bull.'

But still, I said, we've got our heart's desire,
The country has enjoyed a year's ceasefire,
A truce . . .

The woman raised a warning hand
And stopped me short.

'A truce? I understand
That means a respite from hostilities,
A break from violence. Do splintered knees
And shattered arms not count as broken then?
The brokers of this peace are breaking men,
They think the rule of law is something that's
Enforced with iron bars and baseball bats.
I mentioned shit just now. If this is order
The only word with which it rhymes is ordure.'

What you say, I said, is true of course.
But in our situation words divorce
Themselves from truth because their marriage would,
We fear, turn Cana's water into blood,
And serve it up not last of all but first,
And so we hope assault may cure their thirst.
What else is there for us to do but trust
That breaking legs will satisfy their lust
For higher things? And who if not their master
Can preserve us from that worse disaster?
McGuinness is that man. He's in control.
There was a time he'd nod and heads would roll.
But now he's got a kinder stratagem:
His call to arms involves just breaking them.
Of course the boys he's crippled may not cheer,
But still the peace has held for one whole year.
In all that time no one has lost his life.

'Tell that', she said, 'to Frank Kerr's grieving wife.'

Frank Kerr, the Newry postman? Oh well, he
Was only murdered accidentally –
Some lads were nicking letters for a prank

And by mistake they found they'd sorted Frank.
He tried to stamp on them, so, nice and tender,
They marked upon his card, Return To Sender.
It isn't right to blame McGuinness for
That unfortunate mishap, and what is more
To say he could have set our minds at ease
By simply shooting off the robbers' knees
And giving back the dough might tickle us
But make poor Martin look ridiculous.
Remember, too, Republican Sinn Fein,
O Brádaigh's boys, could easily regain
The ground the IRA now occupy
If postmen's widows are in short supply.
There is, as well, the possibility
This iron man is shaping up to be
Another Michael Collins: hard as steel
But capable of bending when a deal
Is offered him. You think this isn't fair?
You think it wrong to say these men compare?
But Collins was a ruthless killer too:
The things that Martin does Mick used to do.
And yet there is a signal difference,
For Collins drew the line at violence
Against civilian targets.

'Try and tell
That to the family of Alan Bell[6] –
An English civil servant, just a clerk,
Who got a bullet on the tram to work –

[6] A Belfast civil servant in Dublin Castle engaged in probing donations
made to the National Loan organised by the Provisional Government.
Michael Collins had him shot in 1920.

To all the widows of the RIC,[7]
To those who suffered the indignity
Of being labelled as a spy, were tried,
Found guilty, hooded, taken for a ride,
Then shot and dumped, a placard tied about
The neck with just two words on it: A Tout.'

Untrue, I said – the Alan Bells he shot
Were fighting with their fountain pens and not
Civilians making sandwiches and tea
For British soldiers. And the RIC?
However Irish, being Royal meant
They were the agents of a government
Which by a vote had lost the right to rule –
Of course, to kill a constable was cruel,
And giving up a job that yesterday
Was honest and that's a crime today
Was hardly practical, not even if
Being slow could quickly make of you a stiff.
So peelers' widows shed their tears in floods?
But they were safe who only peeled their spuds.
And touts? Informers were a real threat
To Collins' volunteers and one he met
Unmercifully. But those who spilled the beans,
As Patsy did, were safe in their canteens.
I know, of course, distinctions such as these
Reveal the wood is full of bloody trees,
But still, though Michael Collins used the axe,
He never wielded it in such attacks
The way McGuinness has . . .

7 The Royal Irish Constabulary.

My voice grew weak,
Trailed off. The spirit woman didn't speak.
Her silence, like her eyes, was full of tears.
I felt the weight of 25 long years
Lie heavy on my tongue, as if I'd known
This quarter of a century of stone
And only learned from it to justify
Soft reasons for the petrified to die.
My sin – so common that we think it good –
Was understanding why I understood.

The value that I thought each life possessed,
The miracle of now made manifest,
Seems now absurd, like thinking that the host
Is changed at Mass into the Holy Ghost.
To rail against our strongest drive, the verve
We have for death, what purpose does it serve?
And even uselessness appears deranged:
Three thousand people died and nothing changed.
Of course this inactivity is thrilling,
Of course the breathing space we've got from killing,
However short it proves, however rough
And ready, is already long enough
For us to act as if there might be things
To think of other than the sufferings
Of strangers in the papers or the news.
And yet their soon-forgotten wounds still ooze
A thickening matter that will not congeal,
And this is what I've come to know and feel,
Without a name for it, is laying waste
To all our hopes for peace: the aftertaste
Of blood, the tang and reek of it, has cursed
Our memory with ghosts. These spirits thirst

For justice. Mouths agape, like famished birds
Who scan the earth, one eye turned heavenwards,
They croak 'Remember how you injured us',
But we are deaf to them and furious
With silence, choosing for our paradise
That hell where human justice is just ice.
Dear spirit, you who knows no barrier,
Forget what we cannot forgive them for,
The guilt we share.

She looked at me, eyes full
Of scorn. 'I know it's not unusual',
She said, 'for people who have been ill-used
To feel they share the blame with the accused.
You seem to think they carry equal weight,
Forgiving those who liked to operate
Without the need for anaesthesia
If they'll forget they have amnesia.
Besides, the longer this ceasefire survives
The closer peace to outright war arrives.
Stick to the facts. The brutal facts are these:
There was no peace when peace meant broken knees,[8]
The de-commissioning of arms a stroke
They pulled, like pulling legs, until they broke,
And pushers died for selling ecstasy,
A drug not in the Provos' pharmacy –
Those youngsters chanting Ebenezer Goode[9]
Soon found they were up to their e's in blood.'

[8] Written on 8 February 1996, the night before the ending of the IRA ceasefire. The line was originally in the present tense.
[9] The name of a Prodigy song, said to be a code for 'Hey Ben, E's Are Good', e's being slang for ecstasy.

I interrupted her. You've changed your tense, I said.
However poor, the peace is here and now.
O tell me why you speak of it as there
And then, as something from the distant past?
She didn't answer me but turned her head,
Her gaze as dark as what it looked upon,
And then a flash of light lit up what was
My window and her sky. Immediately
I heard a bang. What's going on, I asked,
My voice as far away as some lost child's
Beneath a fallen house, my heart a moth
On fire and fluttering within my chest.

She spoke, almost indifferently it seemed:
'Well, is is was. Look out the door,' she said.

How did I open it? And yet I did.
Outside a train was halted on the track.
It lay there, windows blazing, like a long
Unfinished line, a sentence in the dark.
I saw the driver in his cabin lift
The phone and heard him speak: 'I've hit something,'
He said, 'and all the bloody power's gone.'

I closed the door, closed it over like
A leaden leaf of paper printed with
A photograph too horrible to go
On looking at. What does this mean, I asked.
'Find out,' she said, 'turn on the radio.'
I flicked the power switch. 'Here is the news,'
A distant voice, so there and then, announced.
'A bomb has just gone off in London near

A railway station. Two young men are dead,
A hundred people have been hurt, some crushed
By masonry, some cut by flying glass.'

Another night went by, it seemed without
A day between, in which we learned their names.
Two names, as different as black and white:
Inan ul-Haj Bashir, aged 29,
And John Jefferies, about the same – I can't
Remember now, already I forget.
Newsagents both. So that's enough of them.

Canary Wharf is what the place is called.
Canary Wharf! My god, a yellow bird,
A bloody yellow bird, a puffy ball
Of sunny-coloured feathers light as dust
With skinny bones no thicker than a thread,
Yoked to a heavy word, a louring pier
Where once upon a time grain rats would lurk
And scurry through the fog as down the gang-
Way came a sailor from Jamaica, sick
For home perhaps, his only memory of sun
A thumb-sized flash and flit of yellow bird
Inside a cage that dangled from his wrist.

'OK,' she said, 'lay off the fancy stuff.
Stick to the facts. Another bomb's gone off,
It's not the first nor will it be the last,
So now you're back where you began your poem.
The only thing that's new, Canary Wharf,
Is just another place at which the train
Of history has stopped, but not for long,
Another station on a track already full

Of halting names. There is a difference though:
Before this bomb went off a deal was made
With those who planted it. Of course, you'll say
There isn't any link between the two.
You'll say the state of which you are a part
Had taken risks for peace. But think of risk,
Look up the word; it means 'expose to chance
Of injury or loss'. Obey the law
Or else is what a state is founded on.
There isn't any room for chance in that.
In terms of power then the meaning's changed:
The risk of loss becomes a certainty,
For when you take a chance with force you give
Away the thing it is and have to wait
On those you gave it to. The law or else
Declines to optimism and belief:
You hope that they'll be nice. You make a god
Of confidence, and like a first-night bride
You put your trust in being nude for love.
So what's a further sacrifice, or two,
Or three, or four? But then the sun comes up,
You wake and find, good lord, that you've been raped.

'Well, that is what you did, and what is worse
The risk you took was taken not with those
You say you want to be your friends but with
Their enemies. So you deny the link?
Come on! The leader of the Irish state
Stood on the steps outside his office and,
In public view, shook Gerry Adams' hand.
And you're surprised – that hand becomes a fist –
The finger of suspicion points at you!

'Nor is the Irish government alone
In limply offering the palm of peace:
In Downing Street John Major greets John White –
(Of course it happens out of public view –
There aren't any votes in snaps like this)
And talks about the future not the past.
For after all there's nothing to be gained
In opening old wounds – the thirty-nine
That Paddy Wilson felt from John White's knife
Are closed and best forgotten, don't you think?
Besides, there isn't any risk in this –
The 'chance of injury or loss', as far
As Wilson is concerned, is dead and gone.[10]

'So Major shakes a hand that stuck a knife
In someone's neck so long ago. So what?
It didn't happen in your territory.
No matter what you say, what happens there
Is, rightly, out of your control, and so
Don't look to London, look at Limerick,
And, now the gun-smoke's cleared, adjust your eyes
And tell me what you see. Is that a car?'
It is. 'And who is sitting in the car?'
Two guards. 'And what are these two guards up to?'
One's bleeding. 'What about the other one?'

He isn't bleeding any more. 'Because?'
Because he's dead. 'I see, What was his name?'

[10] On 26 June 1973 John White, now a leading spokesman for loyalist
paramilitaries (who have, it must be said, expressed remorse for their
crimes), stabbed to death the SDLP Senator Paddy Wilson and his
companion, Irene Andrews.

McCabe, or Gerry to his wife and friends.
'I see. And no one knows who murdered him?'

We do. 'You do?' It was the IRA.
'I see. And Mr Adams?' He's upset.

'He is?' He is indeed. He says it's wrong.
'How wrong?' He says it's very very wrong.
'I see. And he of course condemns the wrong?'

Well, no. What's wrong does not imply the deed
Was bad, immoral, evil or a sin.
It was instead a fault, a flaw, a lapse,
A blip, a blur, a blot, a sad mistake.

'So terror is an error with a t?'
In Gerry Adams' mouth it is. 'But not
In yours?' I didn't, couldn't, answer her.

'It seems your grief has struck you dumb,' she said.
'That's understandable, considering
A servant of the state, a man exposed
To injury or loss to keep it safe,
Should lose his life to Mr Adams' friends.
It must be hard to think of Gerry-Dead
And then of Gerry-Very-Much-Alive,
The one a ghost exposed to flash and flame,
The other one a guest exposed to light
And printed in a famous photograph.
But still, though Gerry-Dead will not return
To stand upon your leader's steps and smile
And shake his hand, it may console his wife
To know that Gerry-Very-Much-Alive

Is, socially, as welcome as a corpse.
No longer merrying in Merrion Street –
His Filofax has anorexia –
He does what Sinn Fein leaders always did
In Irish history: he stands alone,
Like Ruth, despised amid your alien scorn.'

I quailed beneath her cold, sarcastic gaze.
Well no, I said, it isn't quite like that.
When Gerry-Very-Much-Alive arrives
These days the protocol is awfully strict;
Instead of public smiling on the steps,
He mounts them privately and goes inside
To shake the hands of lesser functionaries
And then he's shown into a separate room.
The Taoiseach's office is off-limits now.

'But when they're in these offices and hear
The call of nature simultaneously
How do they answer it without the risk –
You know the word – of meeting in the jakes?
Perhaps they put aside their differences
And sing The Meeting of the Waters[11] there?
Or is it that, as in my Father's house
There are many mansions, yours is flush
With closet space, and so they're kept apart?
If not, perhaps there's someone keeping nix,
A sort of traffic cop – excuse that word –
Employed to be a Guardian of the Piss,[12]
Ensuring that the Taoiseach's path is clear?'

---

[11] A song by Tom Moore.
[12] The *Garda Siochána*, the title of the Irish police force, translates as 'Guardians of the Peace'.

I didn't answer her. 'Of course,' she said,
That's information you're not privy to.
But tell me this: what happens afterwards?
I guess that Gerry-Very-Much-Alive,
Though grateful for this audience, is like
That character in William Shakespeare's play
Who felt he was 'sick in the world's regard,
A poor unminded outlaw sneaking home?'

Well no, I said. These days when Gerry quits
The offices of government he nips
Around to see his pals in parliament.
He gets a warm, or warmish, welcome there.
The Soldiers of the Rearguard[13] – oops, again –
Surround him at the gates of Leinster House
And listen while poor Bertie talks of peace
And Gerry gravely nods – a nod that's not,
I fear, as grave as Gerry-Dead is in. . . .

'Well, there's your link. In fact, it's more than that,
It is a coupling, a marriage of
Two minds admitting no impediment,
The mark of Cain upon an Abel state
Once prouder of its laws than of its love
For those who threaten it. And all of this
You risked for hope? But now your hope has gone,
It's flown away into the fog as if
It were a bird, a kind of weakling dove
That left the Ark to find an olive branch

[13] The Fianna Fail party is also known as the Soldiers of the Rearguard.

Of future peace. Still waiting its return,
You wonder has it drowned and never think
Perhaps it's not the flood you have to blame
For drowning it but what you sent it for.
Perhaps it didn't drown. Perhaps it burned
Because the olive branch was made of fire.'

This is, I said, too harsh. For half my life
These islands suffered internecine strife.
My being and the state, so long alarmed,
Are like the rhyming scheme I use, deformed.
That hardly matters – crippled as I am,
I know I've got my limp into my poem –
But how can we accept that seeking peace
Should find us stranded in this hate-filled place?
Like Lazarus thrust back into the tomb,
We wait here hoping for a second time
To rise again? That prospect's eating us
The way the eagle gnawed Prometheus.
We feed on hope but hope's a cannibal.

'Don't whinge,' she said. 'Remember, though you're ill,
You have the power that doctors have – say awe –
That tablet stone, the letter of the law.
And what is more the laws you promulgate
Are backed up with the powers of the state.
There's little point in trying to appease
New friends instead of ancient enemies.
You have your health, it isn't you that's sick,
So cut the crap and give them such a kick
Their arses shut, inducing them to shit
Upon themselves instead of stirring it,
And then offend them as they squat and strain

By crying, Constipation Once Again![14]
Eight hundred years of being hard done by
Is long enough and if a jaundiced eye
You cast on them you can be sure your sight is
Not a consequence of hepatitis,
And if you can't be sure, remember please
That certainty's a terminal disease.
So, however Sisyphean, mock
The dogmatists who think their faith's a rock,
Deride its sham and gag upon the bile
That pukes its ring about this septic isle.
Seek peace of course, but don't pretend
That you can make your enemy a friend
Until he's brought to understand that love
Has iron hidden in its velvet glove.'

Instead of anger in my heart exploding,
I felt another sentiment: foreboding.
I fear, I said, this thing has gone too far
For any remedy but civil war,
A time when those convinced they're reasonable
Will think that seeking peace is treasonable.
Nor is this far away: a few attacks
On Dublin and the numbers who cry pax
Will count themselves and quickly know
They'd be hard pushed to fill the GPO.
Tonight I stopped to read the things I wrote
And thought: if someone cut my daughter's throat
Would I, like Jesus, turn the other cheek
And love the murderer, or would I shriek

---

[14] An anthem of nationalism is the song 'A Nation Once Again'.

For blood and want to do to him what he,
His daughter also dead, had done to me?
These fears are real, not paranoid conceits:
When blood is running down familiar streets,
What's inexplicable in Serbia
Looks plain as daylight in suburbia.
I fear that this is what our country craves,
An island famed for its communal graves.

She turned away from me. My gaze was drawn
To what she saw: outside the window dawn
Was giving back the bushes and the trees
Their shadows and their names. By slow degrees
Each leaf defined itself, a sober grey
At first but with the middle of the day
Already hinting at a bluer theme,
And on a single blade of grass a gleam
Of otherwise unseeing sunlight taught
A drop of dew the way that water ought
To sparkle till the moment when its mass
Can't bear it any longer, shining as
It falls. It didn't fall. It trembled there
As if suspended in the morning air
By timelessness, by no desire to be
A simple consequence of energy,
Unused and unavailable, beside
Itself with grief.

I waited for her word
It didn't come. Outside and in were still.
The train had gone. Still powerless, shunted off.
The passengers, alive, somewhere at home,
Asleep and dreaming of disastrous things.

Why had it come and stopped outside my house?
There was no cause, unless it was to show
The awful everywhere of accidence,
Indifferent to every rule but rhyme,
The sometimes coupling of happenstance
With human reason for the sake of it,
And life arising from its opposite.
I felt my poem had reached its end and yet
It seemed that after all I'd failed my muse,
Or even worse, that she had failed herself.
The anger fills my heart, I said, and still
The house is empty too, and nothing's changed.
Is this the way the journey has to end?

She didn't answer me, and yet I heard.
I heard the way that thunder hears itself.
Her eyes were still and yet I saw them move,
I saw the way that lightning sees itself.
Profoundly deaf the one,
The other blind from birth.

And then, and then
I saw the night-long tear that stood within
Her eye grow huge, embreast itself the way
That water does, and with a tearing sound –
The movement was the only noise it made –
Detach itself and fall. A falling star
In miniature, a meteor of dew
And yet the size of sky, it filled the room
And broke and washed the window clean –
For pity's sake. With angry emphasis!
And all its other milder synonyms:
For empathy. Compassion. Clemency.

For tenderness and mercy, sympathy,
For yearning and regret and charity,
And all those words applied to proper names
For pity's sake:
For Bloody Sunday. Aldershot. For Pat
Gillespie and his wife. For Margaret Wright.
For everyone who dies and doesn't know
The reason why, except it's not for love.

She said: 'If not for that for what?
What else is there to give the dead?'
In lieu of answers that was all she had:
An interrogative. But then she added this:
'There's nothing else except
That altogether useless thing,
That surplus to requirements,
Suffering
In silence.'

And so I woke. And for a moment, lost
To time, I thought the world again,
The world before our border hatred, crossed
In love, forgot its ghosts. She vanished then.

May 1993 – May 1998

BRIAN LYNCH

The Kitchen God

I

When you first came we had green queen olives
Marinated in herbed oil with every dish,
Raw coriander sharpening the rich
Soups and curries, cumin speckled breads, cloves —
Their lusty oil seeping into our clothes
From the skin; garlic by the bulb, radish,
Chilli sliced and dangerous to the touch;
Nutmeg wines, gingered teas, cinnamon toast.

You made the whole kitchen yours. Food smelted
You, flesh and hair tinctured, scented in spice,
Your whole body one hot place to be rubbed,
Peeled, primed for the palate, a flavour held
A long time on the tongue, requiring ice
In the mouth to steady your tasters pulse.

II

You brought your fire cooking, translating wood
Gathered at first light — coax, stoke, blow, crackle
Of kindling under the flame, the bubble,
Ooze of sap as a branch burns — into good-
Ness, raw warmth on faces, the fire's given food.
Remember that big black-bottomed kettle,
The first pot of the day's tea, set to boil,
Chappatis, finger made, carob sweet, grilled?

Then, the others coming, couples sleeping
As the fire warmed awake, a lone child drawn

By a smoke-promise drifting through the trees –
And me now, scenting breakfast simmering
Through the house, nudged from sleep, a dream that haunts
All morning like the sharp bloom of brewed leaves.

III

I taught you to make bread. I said, patience,
My love, is the key. Remember the hash
Cookies burnt sugar-bitter, tough, boot-black?
(We had them with tea, they brought visions.)
For those three hours we agreed silence.
By gesture, I showed you – my body, hands
Touch-knowing all over again the craft
Of dough, its textured weight held until learnt.

Moist-warm, rising is the best. *Watch now*
For the elastic flesh to swell. Proving
In darkness under a damp cloth, it grew
Towards the next thump of muscle. Its brown
And woody smell was coming from your skin.
You grew, initiated; love followed.

IV

I thought perhaps you were a sugared fruit
Left long in the sun, those tangy crystals
Surfacing through your flesh to your skin (full,
Washed deep in its perfume). I bit into
The promise and prophecy this flush suit
Like harvest brings, found a nest of wasps tails
That caught and stung my tongue. My quick mouth
    swelled
At the poison, a warning I refused.

But you are plentiful. Always ready
To fall from your branch, roll into my hands.
You give up your surface to the pared white
Raw-ness beneath, my edged fingers heavy
With rapacious love. I forget, burr-blind
In your fragrance, the waiting, hoarded blight.

V

Food-Faggot, Bread-Thief, Hog's-Dinner, Cuckoo,
Sauce-Stealer, Pan-Taster, the Lion's proof
Of majesty picking clean to the hoof
What I've caught, slain, offered up to you.
Tracking delicacies all afternoon,
The last sliver in my dish that soothes
Your appetite fed to your waiting mouth;
Slippery fingers against a sharp tooth.

Something must give. I'm running on empty –
Slim-line, fasted as you soften, fill out.
What was that music you first brought to mind?
L'Après Midi d'un Faune – Debussy. He
Should see you now – A Falstaff, or Faust,
Restless for the hunger in flesh you find.

VI

Darling, I know this craving, loathed desire.
We could name it 'Love', draw the parallel
Of infatuation and disgust – smell
Of stale sex that wets you, stokes a cool fire
From the ashes until you're asking for more.
Yet in waking, the appetite repels
The body from its excesses. And still
You cram a skin-full, load your flesh, perspire.

However, let us balance our dining
With our fucking – crumb the sheets with biscuit
Aperitifs; utilize the kitchen,
Its opportunities for invention,
A tray at the bedside with titbits
Shared between meals to keep the body keen.

VII

Food is your element, our days portioned
Between servings, what waits in cool cupboards,
Jars, bottles, greased wrappings, stacked shelves that hoard
Half-forgotten flavours lying unnamed
In reclaimed honey pots, their pure, ancient
Power a subtle healing packed, known, stored
In the uncracked grain. By rule, you make more
Than needed – supper is always eaten.

You cook while I write, bring cups of dark herb,
Crisp brown toast. Do you remember
When I was pregnant – I loved that red spiced
Soup with lentils, a glob of yoghurt stirred
In, your unleavened bread, salt and pepper
tarting the dough, dipped and sucked. So, so nice.

VIII

A Feast! Who grew the spinach that graces
The salad? You did! Who cultured and tamed
Tomatoes all summer to plush inflamed
Fruit we now hold and admire – faces
Sun flushed as their heavy skins? Traces
Of their flavour linger long. We shall name
them for you – Ruari – Red Faced One – shame
Of sweetness and desire, wantonness!

Satisfied, plump and puffed, drowsy on cheap
Wine, we fill the bed, spill over towards
Dreams; sighs, giggles, tomorrow's half-formed thoughts.
Our bellies, loved one, meet even in sleep,
Pressed close as the pea-green halves of a pod,
Mine, seeded again, growing towards yours.

SARAH CORBETT

Seventy

By now, I suppose,
I should have acquired
the wisdom of age
and gone off to the hills
benign and smiling
like an ancient Chinese,
or taken to the road
with only a staff and tin can,
like an ageing Hindu.

I've always envied people
like that, people in control,
who know who they are
and where they're going;
the sort who decide as infants
to 'dedicate their lives'
to painting, poetry, music,
God, football or whatever,
and never waver.

Not that I'm complaining.
I survived the war.
The girl I really wanted
wanted me. I've travelled
and seen enough of the world
not to want to see any more . . .
It's just that most of the time
I've felt like a trickle of water
flowing downhill. You'd swear

it had a will of its own
as it circumvents obstacles,
pauses, accelerates,
turns this way and that,
but keeps going down
as if nothing can stop it
reaching its end.
Though, of course, it has no end.
Not in that sense.

One day, someone told me,
you'll look back and see
that there was a pattern
all along. I doubt it.
And anyway, to me, that kind
of hindsight is suspect,
like history and biography.
It's seeing faces in the fire
and patterns in the stars.

Besides, it's getting late;
and here, on the threshold
of senility, there's no sign
of any emerging pattern.
And as for dying, I imagine
it will be like walking
into a Rothko painting –
a large fuzzy blank doorway
leading to nothing.

L.R. ROGERS

The Lost Island of St Kilda

I am a stranger in the crowd
I am a man upon the sea
And I must leave the city loud
And build a boat to carry me –

Beyond the Western Isles away
To live by wind and sail and hand
Three hundred miles from Mingulay
Westward, far beyond all land –

And steer for that sheer granite stack
That echoes with the seabird's cry
And to the ruined kirk go back
Where all my fisher fathers lie

And set the rickled stones upright
Where first my mother cradled me
And crooned to us through many a night
Safe from the dark and deafening sea

I was a boy in this stark land
My barefoot youth was wild and free
Let no man seek to understand,
Whose home is not the sky and sea.

Historical footnote: in August 1929 the British Government evacuated the centuries-old but dwindling community of St Kilda, judging that life on that remote and barren island was no longer sustainable. The St Kildans lived out the rest of their miserable existence on the Scottish mainland, never ceasing to mourn their loss.

TONY HORWOOD

Atlantis Season

'This is Atlantis season again'.
'Independent on Sunday' – (11 January 1998)

As we wake on this unseasonally bright spring-like
January day, Russian academics have abandoned
their maps of the stars to seek Plato's mythical lost
   city.

It is at once flat, rectangular yet high, circled by
mountains; has a drainage canal and strange metals.
One sparkles like a red fire. Its kings hunted bulls for
   sport.

Famously, it is thought to drift under the wild tides
off Land's End or lie in a flooded Turkish plain; on the
   shores
of a Bolivian lake. Literary heroes have stepped into
its sunken ruins. We too may have sunbathed in the
   vanished outline
of its beaches, snorkelled above its battlements and
   spires;
glanced idly at excavated paintings of bulls fighting
with men then tramped past to find the nearest bar.

Now this bed is a sunken ruin, littered on your side
with sports' pages and our daughter competes for your
   attention
while the digits on the clock sparkle like red fires.

I try to find Atlantis in the dregs at the bottom of my mug
but tea-bags have put an end to mysterious speculation
and there is a day to get through before we can read the
    papers
properly; a midland city outside, rising above itself.

PAM THOMPSON

Piano Lessons: Sarajevo

Scene: Sarajevo, mid-day
Tempo: Grave

The Piano Teacher:
The keys of the piano are black and white spies
which betray these now feeble fingers. If I
cross over that border, my tongue
will give me away too. I have become this other
woman, this bearer of secrets. The streets are
deserted, the buildings I once knew as close as
friends are enemies. Windows are eyes
which signal regret.

The Student:
Only when the sound of explosions
drifts off behind the hills and
the sirens stop their pulsating rhythm
is it quiet enough to come up from the
basement to the dangerous room
where light can act as insidiously as
a landmine. I wait for the tap tap
of her danger on the door.

Teacher:
Memory explodes if not carefully tested, fingers
brush cobwebs from the reflections of happier times,
when light poured its golden notes through
the clean windows and the music, the music —

much has been forgotten in a short time, pushed
down below the surface while light rages
above and through the thin cracks.

Student:
A note, cautiously explored: is there anyone out there?
two notes in slow apology, parenthesis: is it
safe? three in quick succession like mice
scurrying across the prison floor: risk
is everything. Play by memory
by what can be remembered when the streets
were adagios of life, buildings solid
as bars of music, when laughter and gaiety
glissaded through the air, water and milk
came to the door on time, the gas stove
puffed a pleasant plume of blue flame.

Teacher:
It's warm and sunlight accompanies her
nervous frets. What is music without war?
I'm so used to walking the streets, it's like
walking between bars of music, my mind
constructs sonatas to the cacophany
of bombs, plays nocturnes at night to
the whistle of falling meteors. I dodge
between overturned cars, shortcut through
the ruined stubble of libraries and
bakeries. Don't be nervous, dear, it's life,
it's music we are playing.

ALLAN B. SERAFINO

Emir

Emir, the quietest of men
did God knows what on a Trebevič hillside
in t-shirt and trainers, to gain the objective
and take the gun. Then

found a Serb lying five days in a cave
who'd drunk dew, and prevented his platoon
fulfilling their passion. Carried him, femur protruding,
one day back to barracks. Was brave,

missed a 1,000 Deutsche handout
from the Merc-driving general,
and returned to his sweetheart
on his hands through the tunnel, gave out

bags of sugar to stick-thin people
who stopped him, fascinated, in the streets
before dumping the rest and himself
on his lover's mum's doorstep. His trouble

being simplicity. And saw later
the exchanged prisoner
on the other channel
talk of beatings and torture

at the hands of some Muslims.
Emir got his despised/cherished certificate
for bravery/humanity, but remembers well
the false tone of the thankful him.

CHRIS HURFORD

The Gospel Singer Testifies

When she spoke, I looked down
the way I would if she'd begun undressing
before everyone, not to entertain
but to show things about ourselves
we knew to cover. So aware that beside me
a Jewish friend listened – or didn't –
to her praise of Jesus.
I wanted to signal, 'We're not all like that.'
But my friend is, we are, all like that:
having something we'd get naked for
before a whole group of people.
That is, if we're lucky. So my body heard
before I did, with tears at the corners of my eyes,
as the words that had begun in song *Thank you, Jesus!*
dissolved back into song, or a finer
distillation, and the singer closed her eyes,
Thank you! bent like a bowstring,
shot forth her nakedness to save me.

SUSAN DONNELLY

News for the Class Anoraks

'The modern man should have everything in his house constructed since the year of his birth' –

> Whynne J. Bassett-Lowke in *Ideal Home*, 1927

At the last count there were 329 members
of the Bassett-Lowke Newsletter – cognoscenti
of 'O' gauge model railways, not just any
old locomotives, rolling stock or tenders;
these are as exact as what they represent:
a four-wheeled tin-plate Brake Van (vgc),
a Exley blood and custard coach (with seats),
a boxed and Standard Scale 'Pacific' (mint).

Those in the know can read between the lines:
a pre-war world that smells of oil and steam,
where ladies made of lead wait on the platform
with their hat-boxes and ask porters the time.
Each figure has its own stand and station,
each knows the proper form – how to address
the other, bearing in mind their rank and class,
the correct way to convey the correct information.

The badly Xeroxed text is smudged but true,
a recipe for what the real world lacks –
the signal certainty of shining tracks
which reach beyond horizons where the new

threatens like thunderheads. The Bassett-Lowkies
tidy their layouts, while outside the blur
of the world hangs like painted sack and loofah
against the duck-egg blue of hardboard skies.

JULIAN TURNER

The Tile Setter

JOHN P. DONNELLY (1901–1995)

I

When he heard that the others
were planning to tar and feather
the Protestant neighbor girl
who loved a Black and Tan soldier,
he ran, because of who he was
and would be for ninety-four years,
over the back fields to warn her.
He was the quiet brother, a camouflaged
gunrunner during the civil war,
who passed messages along the deep hedge lanes
left notes in the crook of a tree.
Everything local, personal. He'd show
his American grandchildren the IRA medal
kept in a desk drawer, then talk of how,
outside his childhood door,
was 'the biggest field in the world'.

II

For one who had learned,
in a new country, to set
tile, learned how to fit
corners, cut each smooth square
into place, round the whole
with the curved border tile; to a man
with his own thoughts doing this,

his dreams and absorbed calculations:
bank account, house, first child
a daughter who fit his arms,
for such a person, what of the crash
in the big, strange country, the Thirties'
great downslide, harsh shattering, loss
of customers, house gone, second child coming,
wife's stony eyes, all the tiles
rubbling down and the tile dust blinding?

III

When his daughter-in-law first met him
he was coming in from his shift
at the Railway Express,
where he'd labored for twenty-five years.
He stumped off his boots
in the back hall – it was December, and snowing.
'You can come right in, John,'
his wife called, 'She's a regular girl.'
He came in, wearing workclothes, his face drawn,
very pale, held out his hand in welcome.
He was all bent inward in those years,
as though tons of boxes and parcels
had been lowered, one by one,
onto his shoulders at the station.
Like the medieval Celtic trials
to prove poets: that they bore
in a pit, under a testing of stones.

IV

Then, in early old age, he finds
the falling-down little house he can fix over.
Rooms that, once cleaned, cry out

for tile, tile everywhere:
above kitchen counters, up the stairs,
a riot in the bathroom, lining the basement shower.
Once that's all set, he goes out
on early spring mornings – he's retired now –
to yard sales, brings back
small tables of every shape, just waiting
to be tile-covered. Blue, cream, brown-speckled,
dusted with gold, they fly off
as wedding presents, gifts to nieces.
There are always new patterns.
Under each table he paints
a huge shamrock, 'John P. Donnelly', the date.

V

'Maureen,' his whispered protest, 'I'm still not dead. . . .'
He's off-schedule, impatient. He told his daughter
yesterday he'd not live past midnight.
Now here's the city sun, filled with haze,
coming through dull hospital curtains.
Down Cloone's main street it would pour
clear honey till ten at night . . .
He's let so much go:
the hard marriage, little house, apartment
full of trailing plants and Irish tea towels,
big TV for watching Notre Dame.
He's left his zinnia garden,
planted along the parking lot. That design
of colors. Left his canopy bed.

SUSAN DONNELLY

A Lazarus Triptych

The carp lie torpid in the winter lake,
buried in mud beneath a lid of ice.
The frozen twigs creak in the wind, and ache
with swollen knots of buds to break and splice
the tender bark. Closed in a carapace
of stippled gold and emerald, the moth,
its coffin painted with its future face,
waits to shake out its wings like new-dipped cloth.
The crocus, crumpled in its shrivelled corm,
sleeps out the harshness of a shrieking storm.

So Lazarus lay, confined within the rock,
swaddled and bound, where icy darkness curled
round death-stilled limbs, and no releasing shock
set free a desert spring to spray the world
with bright amazement. Like a silent seed,
a child unborn, unquickened, there he rested.
His time was not yet come. No use to plead
with God, his sisters knew. Their faith was tested
by knife-sharp grief, incredulous dismay –
that vivid life quenched in a single day?

Martha, the elder, with her practised hands
brought spices, myrrh and aloes; neatly wrapped
and packed his corpse with tight-drawn linen bands;
contained corruption, kept decay entrapped.
Summoned by neighbours to an awkward birth,
or when breath rattled in a dying throat,

she thanked God for the harvest of the earth,
ripe figs to store, soft wool to weave a coat;
yet now her brother set her hardest task,
sealed like last summer's olives in a cask.

. . . 'If you were there, my brother had not died . . .'
Yet there he lay, irrevocably dead.
But her exhausted memory still tried
to form an image . . . loaves of leavened bread,
not for the festivals, but every day,
kneaded, as she had worked his lifeless flesh,
and left to rise, out of the children's way,
a common miracle, but always fresh –
that bread of life, warm with its new baked crust . . .
'Lord, in my blindness, teach me how to trust.'

Mary's slim fingers smoothed the ointments in,
as she had done so many times before,
salving the sore awareness of her sin,
when townsfolk's tongues dismissed her as a whore.
The even rocking motion of her palms
had soothed taut muscles, lifted stubborn pain,
dissolving it away with fragrant balms,
to leave men vigorous and freed from strain,
but now the body she anointed lay
as unresponsive as a lump of clay.

The half-formed phrases flickered in her brain . . .
To yield its sweetness, spikenard must be crushed,
bruised like our hearts with sorrow . . . Once again
she whispered to her sister, but was hushed,
thinking of how the last man she had eased
with comfort for his soiled and blistered feet,

had let her sit and learn from him, well pleased,
though Martha muttered, 'Still, we have to eat!',
and taught her how they make a perfect whole –
body in balanced harmony with soul.

There was some old Greek story he had heard
a girl who found her brother in the dust,
and gave him burial, quite undeterred
by the king's threats of violence or lust,
even of death . . . so she would do as much for this poor
body. What she could bestow
through tender reverence and expert touch,
patiently she would give, secure to know
her brother's spirit, quick and bright as flame,
leaping to meet the source from which it came.

'Lord, by this time he's stinking – three days dead . . .'
But time spins backwards on its crazy wheel;
The gift unwraps itself; to Martha's dread
the bandages unravel, to reveal
a clear smooth skin, and blinking newborn eyes
a vulnerable forehead, tumbled hair
recalling nothing, yet immensely wise;
the cloying scents disperse in sunny air
and pale new light, faintly foreshadowing
that greater Resurrection time will bring.

SUSAN REYNOLDS

House of the Two Sisters

SOINTULA, BRITISH COLUMBIA,
1909

Birches sigh like running
water – not this water.
The steel straits, the marble island out
there, between riptide and regretful
ebb. Blue as a gun barrel on a June day.

You opened each
page of the strange newspaper
creamy wings lifting
further to freedom before
you would flatten them, paste them on
another flank

of new wall: How we worked
together. Our wall stands
proud as plumbob and square could make it, true
as the pale determined forests
of home, of Suomi. Our little Finland
here, this island, our smaller
sanctuary between headlands, beyond the fists
of north wind.

Two sisters, all the others said, *How
can these poor children manage?*

I was twenty-nine, too old
to marry.
You were twenty-six.
The one so close between us
an absence now.

I bargained – they said –
like a Russian. *This board will not do.*
I said I'd have no splits, no knots,
worms have been here
and here. Cut another.

I bowed to learning
grew expert straightening the first
three hundred nails I bent.
You found the meadow
beyond, trees and white stars in the grass
so green we had no word, the stars
from a botany unknown.

The dictionary burned. Like children
we spoke to these English in their paradise
of greed.

Now I wander
from your meadow. I see you still,
turning, dappled
in leaf shadow, your old straw hat
forgotten on a branch,
your cloakroom.

Look! a victory
in Saint Petersburg! The paper
four years old, never mind, from Helsinfors

we called it then, the Swedish capital
but Russians were the threat
even then. We said it quietly, and louder:
Helsinki.

Helsinki.
And Suomi, our star
rose in the west, our brother
lost in the east.

Too late, perhaps
the Tsar took him, at least
his stubbled sergeant reeking of garlic
called us Lapps and witches
belched crude
jokes of mating with the wind or red
stags. We were not herders, we knew
the birches and quiet water, our brother
best of us all.

Why did he not run?
As we ran
from the blue carbine, the sight of it
in his hands. He held it stiffly
broken from his lashings,
not from his pride.

They sent him far
beyond the map, beyond Port Arthur
our little captain broken to private
lost
a spent cartridge

a square of hardtack
nothing of value.

His spirit, cat-eyed
will find this meadow. On cold nights
when dry sticks rattle I think
we're closer
anyway, east from Vladivostok
south from Alaska
far from all gold fields
thank providence.

In Sointula
here in harmony, our chord
may speak again. We were three. Two
sisters remain. One soaring after
her flighty pages, her plan
for perfect peace
the brotherhood of man.
Another biting down
on nails and unsaid doubts.

Sointula. They burden this small island with a name
too big for brothers
even sisters. Harmony?
Why not Utopia? Why not Heaven?
But your passion beats upward
your homely pages fly east
to Canada. *No! It's in our reach!*

Not in our grasp – this
I do not say. You builders of perfection
are so helpless with bent nails.

I kneel to dreams, hammering
another straight. Each blow
the dream will grow
more likely.

You capture
Saint Petersburg, pursue Helsinki
across a foreign meadow.

I stir your drying glue, tomorrow's breakfast
unless we turn
a profit soon. Calves, grain, weaner pigs
two hundred miles to market by open boat —
and then the great fire, our ruin.
The dreamers never reckoned
we could starve.

We didn't. Whale clan
women came to give us dry fish
berries, roots, clams, fish grease
fish fillets
fish cheeks
fish.
We reeked.

They helped us dig the cookstove from the ashes
of Harmony, and went silent
paddles dipping silver
home.

You lay Helsinfors – Helsinki – flat
between my green uprights, stand back
admire. And that is all of Finland we have

to warm this house against
an Aleut wind.
Next you grasp Canada.
Vancouver World, an oxymoron. You frown
as your slender finger finds
eight columns of land for sale. *Such greed!*

Already you'd forgotten greed also brought us
here for liberty, for land
in no man's name.

Yet your smile snags
silken on a page of Paris
finery you'll never see. My sister socialist
leagues from society, my sister in fashion
with your frayed straw hat fallen
to the grass and stars.

This house will stand. Another sister
will come and lift a shutter,
read Canada and Suomi on the walls
under their whitewash
hold this nail
its bend, its straightening
know calluses from dreams.

S.W. MAYSE

Waking

It is morning. Hop up now
frog of old Wellingtons. It is May.
There are mountains of helpfulness
on your horizon. The mudflaps call
pitter patter over the landscape.
The day is caking up on you.
Hop up and listen! The footpaths
sing marsh marigolds, splashy
and dew throated, bramble in nailpolish.
Skip through the slick of it,
unfloppy, green-eyed. Be eager today.
You are a frog. Find the spring in you.

ANDREW BRENNER

Metamorphosis

First came a taste for meat
and odd bursts of irritation
like an itch along her spine.

Then she lost the urge to speak.
She'd curl up in the back room,
whole days at a time,

and at night she'd sleep-walk
through the house, nudging
at the windows and the doors,

lifting her face to the draughts,
listening to a wood louse
scratching under the apple bark.

She wondered at sofas and knives,
and no longer knew the meaning
of *milk* or the colour red,

what *hot* was and *cold*, and *nice*,
why some things shone and some
were dark, and why the baby cried.

RUTH SHARMAN

Anne Boleyn

'I am come hether to accuse no man, nor to speake any
thyng of that, whereof I am accused and condempned to
dye, but I pray God save the king and send him long to
reygne over you, for a gentler nor a more mercifull prince
was there never: and to me he was ever a good, a gentle
and soveraygne lorde.'

1527
That afternoon I stripped
to my underwear and lay
fingering each moment.
His visit had been unannounced
but in his wife's chamber I was the one
he danced with. He couldn't
make his eyes leave me.

The following evening I remember the floor
covered in cloth of silk, his black velvet slippers
on the lilies' embroidered gold. I knew
when he unmasked it was my future I'd see.

The gifts started: emerald rings, bows, arrows,
his picture set in bracelets, linen, rich furs,
saddles and harnesses, rubies, diamonds,
pillions in black velvet. He took me to the Tower,
filled my arms with gold plate,
fine black satin.

1532

It was the rain in Calais,
insistent for two weeks,
like his fingers at my bodice,
his jewels at my throat.
The puddles soaked up five years of resolve,
ran it into the brown and swollen sea.

1533

He married me secretly that winter,
unclasped my desire like never before.
His square bed saw me remove
each last thread of gold, thread of silk
till only jewels remained, and the king
created a thousand heirs a night.

Before the coronation fifty barges
took me to the Tower. It was May.
Five months pregnant I wore
rich cloth of gold, and for Westminster
purple velvet trimmed with ermine.
My hair I left loose, but on that day
not even the wind dare disturb me.

I had the peacocks removed before the birth.
I never liked their eerie cries.
Lady Lisle sent me peewits.
My husband planned a tournament and a pageant.
He selected the names Henry and Edward.
I had an altar set up in my room,
read the Bible in French.

He blamed my womb for the daughter.
By Michaelmas he had a mistress,
had taken her to his square bed.
He would strip other women now,
make sure the rumours reached me.
Suddenly I wanted the peacocks back, to hear
their cries rather than my own.

1536
The January Catherine died I wore yellow.
Elizabeth I dressed in orange satin.
Pregnant again, I had my lying-in chamber
made yellow ochre and told the Henry inside me
how he was longed for, how he could save
his mother, save his father
from signing her death warrant.
The day after the funeral,
as if to punish me for false sunshine,
he struck me with pain, came out
as deformed as my future.

On the second day of May they came for me.
Holding our daughter I pleaded with Henry,
reminded him of the May we first danced,
our summer progresses, Calais,
how he used to watch
if the wind lifted my hem,
his letters of love, his great agony
whenever we were parted, how
wherever he was he belonged to me.
But the look in his eyes was as though
we no longer had humanity in common.

Three hours in the barge to the Tower.
I heard the water and when I closed my eyes
a pavanne. In the same lodgings
as before my coronation I looked
in the mirror. I was not yet thirty.

What could I do but laugh then weep,
weep then laugh. My sweet brother
died because of me. Of my father and mother
I heard nothing. I never let myself think
they believed I was a witch,
believed the incest, the adultery.
I was Anne, little Anne. Had father not kept
the letter in which I promised
I would strive to please him?
Seven years old. Suddenly I remembered
clavichord lessons with Hendrick.
Suddenly I remembered the executioner
trying out his new platform,
his pockets for the £24.

May the 19th
7am. A watery breeze.
My window open
as I dress and pray.
My speech is ready.
My hair is dark.
I choose black damask
with an ermine mantle of white.
For my head
a cap of linen.

HELEN FARISH

Errantries

Slip on your lobster hauberk with the breast ridge of blue
    steel,
Hang out a pouting casque beside the saddle-bow
and slowly jog into the rains.

Ride over three pearled fields, or one good mile of heather,
with Rosinante's fetlocks threshing the tall brome;
drubbing together like a mace's down strokes.

Look out for towers; ivyed and silent in the dusk;
a cave, a ditch, a hollow oak or, if you must, a heath;
between the hours of dog and wolf.

Sleep in full armour. Difficult enough!
But also try to dream of ruffled silk,
pale hands, red roses and blue eyes.

Mount up at dawn, stiff-limbed and shivering,
point north and tremble. Compass this.
Then ride home to your central-heating.

Download the chills of night;
add forests, fairy hills, cash-counters
and a white face, glimpsed in dreams.

Click Rosinante to her binary stable,
save it, then exit; turn your mind to other things.
Hoover the front room, clear the breakfast table.

And once upon a motorway, somewhen or other,
you'll pull in for a breather or a snack,
and suddenly one word you'd never thought of –

certainly a word you'd never go out looking for –
will break in on you through a crack between the worlds.
You'll know.

Because the moon will be before you at the check-out;
with a basket full of icicles, and frosty smile.
Now, while she counts her money . . .

Whisper the word across her shoulder!

Watch her glow gold; and melt until she's sweet at honey.
(Though get it wrong and you could be arrested!)
This is your first quest anyway. Run through it at your
      leisure.

Now, dig out shield, lance, sword, mouse, modem, or
      whatever.
Make back-up copies. Surf the web. Check forecasts of the
      weather;
and whistle up the groom to bring the horses.

PAUL F. COWLAN

Not a Worm Moves

on his allotment not a worm moves without permission
each lettuce keeps nine inches from its neighbour
no more, no less
and an onion, failing to grow orthodox, symmetrical
is humiliated, and dies

at home, he is careful to put his boots where allocated
to fold the toilet paper just so, before use
(although she cannot see this)
and to sit only on the designated chair, holding the
      newspaper
at the right angle, thinking only the right thoughts

she, while looking for some misdemeanour to be
      mentioned
conscious that the rot spreads quickly if not nipped in the
      bud
yet wonders how this worm became his slave, and then his
      master
and contemplates the key or apple that could take them
from prison into Paradise

JOHN GILHAM

A Beat in the Palm

They celebrated when he
declared himself head of
state, feasting through
the day and into night.
Noises in shops, market
places filled funeral
parlours, whore houses,
hospitals, in the capital.
People pressed on their
horns, aroused those that
dozed off under trees or
canopy.

Citizens converged on the
front of government house
to hear for themselves the
General's words, how, and
in what manner he toppled
the ex president with his
bunch of paratroopers.

Outside the city soldiers
stood guard against others.
They brandished rusty rifles,
plunged bayonets into the
wind with infernal fury.
They marched up, down, their
guns pointed, fun-like but

fearful as they demonstrat-
ed with mimicking cries the
dying moment of a president.

Servants threw the garments
of their masters into the
air and hardened criminals
danced closely with wives
of judges, lawyers. Bakers,
shoemakers, swapped aprons,
butchers and doctors rolled
themselves in each other's
urine. Gardeners carried
garlands of sweet scented
flowers while bragging mer-
chants offered strung sheep
eyes to men and mare's milk
to newly born babies.

The orphanage keeper worked
herself into a real frenzy.
Words! Words touched hearts
and heads of many revellers.
They sang cheerily the song
'Deliverance' and extended
the joyful mood to 'we de
masses from now must over-
come, honey bees we were
meant to be, not boisterous
clowns who cannot see.'

The scene seemed set, even
Amzon the armless, legless,

torso of a man had himself
prettied up with rows of
tiger teeth and monkey paws
around his neck hoping to
get a woman. He too latched
on to the chorus of de masses,
de masses, added, no tuxedos
today, we have the right way.

On the forecourt harp play-
ers excelled with countless
ancient lingering melodies.
Dancers, drummers, spread the
grounds. Patiently people
listened to spirit-catchers
pleading with the ancestors.
Softly came few answers, some
burdened the oracle with rage,
demands too many, like wild
birds in a cage.

Hunters and herdsmen came
from the forests and fields,
saturated by a dream, energy
flowed to suit their coming.
The moon and the sun almost
kissed and night hawks flapped
wings perched on government
railings. They chirped along
with the sonneteers. The wood
cutters kept a fire burning,
women, warm, cuddled children
as night was falling.

The fire brigade, the taxi
drivers, ambulance workers,
police, all pledged their
allegiance to this gallant
leader. From a window I saw
and heard everything. Winds
blew in my direction brought
tears, joy, and I witnessed
the crowd of human toys.

A valiant young trooper
had arrived with a beat
in the palm of his hand,
announced by way of pro-
clamation that it was the
heart of the dead leader,
a drunken soldier seized
his wrist to devour him
forever.

From a platform the presi-
dent poured his conscience
to the nation, bellowed for
radio and television. His
long speech bound attitude
needed to change a country
based on servitude.

Ah! a truck pulled in
with the entrails of the
tyrant. A pack of hungry
terriers lay in wait to feed
upon bristle and muscles

with vengeance, a torn fat
vein will end thirty years
of pain.

I didn't wait the outcome,
quietly I walked to my bed,
a head full of proverbs, I
wept. In between, I heard the
singing once more – De masses,
de masses. My hands covered
my face when I began wonder-
ing who'll have the opportun-
ity to be the next judge of
cruelty.

T-BONE WILSON

Rafting Rise

'They would never believe what we could tell them. There ain't a damn soul a'livin' around here that can back up my tales. They's all dead now.'

L. Blackman Davison, Ohio Co., KY, 1978

We came to the end
of cutting and hauling
having had enough
of wet bottoms
and yokes of oxen
up to their knees in mud,
straining at the logs.

We came to the end
of cutting
and hauling
when we saw the
great white oak
larger than four of us
could reach round.

We waited
for the rise,
when Rough River
would swell up
and fill itself,
two-thirds bank,
not too high.

We waiting beside the
cold water for the rushing
creeks to empty themselves, and
measured time by the river's rise
and by the sledge's swing
as we beat together
our raft with pins and poles.

When we first
felt the water and
the current took us,
the logs moaned,
my stomach cut loose
from my body and
floated free with the raft.

Holding the steering oar was
like fighting a great fish
when you have
to give it line
lest it break away,
yet try to keep it
free from stumps and snags.

The raft pulled and yawed
like it was alive,
but it was the river
that lived. We rode
on its back at the mercy
of cold water
and colder wind.

It was then I cursed
Robin who'd come
by that November day
when my father and I
were firing tobacco
in the barn.
'Hey Bill, let's go
for the rafting rise.
We'll cut our trees
and ride them all the
way to Evansville
and sell them,
then lie up in the
Acme Hotel and Oyster Bar,
with its $2.00 rooms
and fifty cent whores.'

So I left my father
and the curing weed
and went across the
river and engaged in
cutting and hauling logs.

Now on the rising
stream, my hands
frozen to the oar,
I listened as the river
roared at Falls-of-Rough
hiding around a bend.

The first logs rode over
then dipped down

into the white water
rushing below the dam.
Robin was up to his
knees while I was
lifted high. The raft
groaned like someone
on a rack, but
the pins held and
we floated free.
Robin's pants froze and
the wind passed through
my clothes like a knife.

At Livermore we
reached the Green
and stopped awhile
to join our raft
to others' –
Dewey's, Henry's
and Ed's.

The Marshal came down
to our camp and
warned us off from town,
but Dewey gave him
a bottle and we all
got drunk, forgetting
about the Green
rising up beside us
and the cold
entering our bodies
through our sodden clothes.

That night I dreamed
a late dream
of the warm barn
and the sweet smell of smoke
and curing leaf, but awoke
cold and sick, here
on the frozen bank.

Five of us
now cut loose our
raft of a thousand logs
and headed down the Green.
If I had thought that once
we navigated the Rough
and jumped its dams
and missed the rocks
at Fishtrap and the Narrows
and joined with other rafts
and then entered the broader Green,
if I had thought that
we had passed the worst,
I had not felt the
power of the Green
in full flood.
Chafing in my mother's kitchen
I could not have believed
how the wind could strike you
fair at 5 below
out on the open water.

In the first night's tie-up
we learned the true
nature of the raft's

weight and the current's power.
In the late winter light
Henry took the skiff
and rowed off to get
a line on a
maple up ahead.
The tree gave way
and almost swamped
his little boat.
Three times he tried,
the third tree held.

Dewey wrapped
our end around
the checking port
when, slowed by the cold,
his hand
fed itself
to the hungry rope
just as the barge
swung against the current.
The frozen rope snapped
taut, hard as iron,
and Dewey's hand
dropped onto the deck,
cleanly cut as
by an axe.
He dropped too,
his face as white
as the sycamore
that held and drew us
back against the bank.

We wrapped his arm
to stop the blood and
laid him in our little hut.
But we could not stop for him,
and cut the rope
for the river was on the rise
and Rumsey dam roared up ahead.
The river ran high,
but the big dam held
its place and made
a falls that turned
the river white.
Our bow dropped down
and disappeared.
Robin and Ed scrambled
toward me,
up the sloping deck.
Henry and I
held on
to the oar
while the stern
reared up in the
frozen air. Again
our good hickory
poles and pins
held tight, though
the raft made
an awful sound.

We ran that day and
night while Dewey
moaned in the shed.
The river devoured

its banks and
spread into the fields.
I ate at the oar
wrapped in a
frozen quilt, the
current beating
beneath my feet.
No one spoke
the second day
as we watched
for the Spottsville bridge
waiting around a bend.
Everything was speeded up
though the river
had grown so broad
that it hardly
seemed to move.
Then we saw
the bridge's piers
cutting the water
like a knife.

The raft turned
 in the current
though four of us
struggled at the oars.
We hit
the center pier
broadside
and hung
just a moment
while the pins
flew out like shot

and the bow
sheered off
with a splintering sound.

Robin, who hung
on the forward oar,
looked startled
then was gone,
while we swung
free and went on down,
our stern become our bow.

The bow logs kept
us company, as we
were swept along.
We entered
the mouth of the Green
and saw
the great Ohio
before us
like a sea,
but could not stop,
caught by the falling
Ohio drawing
the rising Green.

Helpless we turned
in the current.
I feared we might
miss Evansville entirely
and be swept on to Cairo,
but the *Water King*,
prowling for rafts

caught in the
river's sudden fall,
threw us a line
and towed us
to Angel Landing
in the mouth
of Pigeon Creek.

We thawed ourselves
for a week
in Evansville's
warm embrace.
Though Dewey
had not his hand
nor Robin
his life,
it was only 1914
and the trees still
were endless, stretching
through the bottoms
far beyond our sight.

JOE SURVANT

Blind Man's Mouse

There are things I don't say.
Roofs in the rain,
a seagull's legs on the sky-line.
I can't translate these hieroglyphs
for fear of hurting.

Put your hands on my face.
Do you care if I'm beautiful?
Something should flow
from the bowl of the skull
to the fingers.

I'm a breathing warmth
you feel in your stubble,
not your ideal. You told me once
she'd never marry a blind man.

When you're drunk we quicken,
night making us equal
flowering with hands
until the dark root stirs.

We don't touch all day
except when I'm guiding.
Two good animals, moving together,
I'm yoked and wifely.
My fault if you stumble,
twinned like a tree that could kill
if it toppled.

Your hurt white eye indicts me.
Once you could see.
Now I'm an absence
moving about in the room.
You are marooned
with the Talking Clock.
I can't complete you.

The glass eye slips in easily
over the socket,
part of your armoury,
curved shell a bluey green
for me to dream into.

A long way down
under its cup
you remember blue.

JILL BAMBER

Anon

What a relief to find my name
means nothing to that man!

Like Dreyfus,
my decorations were torn off.
I was held up to universal scorn,

shoved out into the world
without a cloth.

Now, as I edge along the windy street,
keeping my head well down,
I find that, after all, no one is looking.

The headlines
are about something else;
I wouldn't trade
with anyone at present in their sights.

Flayed, gasping,
though I can't change my habits overnight,
I start relaxing.

Nothing is here except the street, and buildings,
dark, overpowering, tall.
They've seen it all.

MERRYN WILLIAMS

Goldfish

He swims in a bowl full of lukewarm white water
Close to the edge, and just under the rim
Of the glass, which reflects the gold scales of his armour
Showerproof and tight fitting, the rain won't get in.

He swims all the time, yet he never gets wetter
And nobody asks 'where on earth have you been?'
Though he races around he will never get better
At getting to know a tail he's never seen.

Water washes you out, there's a hint of a cold shower
I feel, as I slurp on my brown tea and toast,
Trying to forget the salt tears on my mirror
Rusting away the face I loved the most.

A. GRANT

The Artist's Model Daydreams

AFTER GIACOMETTI

My head is a spoon that dips and scoops
fine sugar from a china bowl, remembers
sherbet ochre tongues and the stain on the
tip of a finger shrivelled with sucking.

My face is a flower that turns with the sun
sneaks a look from the edge of a tarmac square,
remembers the scrape and bounce of fivestone chalks
worn smooth and round with playing.

My back is an S that aches on a stool, remembers
the scale of ascending C where thumbs go under,
the broken key and the ring of a fender, bruised
in simple time, by a poker's four-four beating.

My legs are a long case clock, a pendulum pair
that swings and remembers great aunt afternoons
the rub of a cut-moquette settee, a glimpse
of a beaded muslined jug, and ticking.

SUSAN UTTING

Cheetahs

He crouches in the kitchen staring out
across the courtyard at the cheetahs playing
with padded paws up there by moonlight on
the roof, their backs arched high, their hairless hides
pulsing with lipstick spots against royal blue.
He turns his head and sniffs. Did something move?
Like a spring he lurches to the table top
where, huge and marble-veined, one red, one silver
and one the colour of a bone, three eels
with pools of liquor lapping at their gills
decay. The staff forgot to put them out
for dinner. All gone off . . . No. One's alive
(or is it just his nose wrinkling with sorrow
at what's been lost?). It seems as if the body
he thought was dead twitches, shudders, stops.
He sighs and slurps some water from his bowl,
collapses on his bed. The moon's dropped off.
He yawns and scratches, making fur fall out.
He wants to be a cheetah. Corridors
away the porter turns a lock. No chance
he'll say good night. Tomorrow might be better.
Fortresses make a dog depressed and sick.

BARBARA NORDEN

A Way Out

Never never in all my life have I
slipped through the floorboards avoiding
the splinters and poured myself out through the
    pipes
insulation and lagging, the brush
of the mushrooms. What will I do if I find out
the slime of a snail when I wander
is all that remains of my mind? Nothing.
Nothing is left of my life.

Never never in all my life have I
launched myself out from the window,
flapping my wings made of bedsheets, scanning
the earthscape of eyeballs and fallen
geraniums. What will I do if the swell of the
current, the puff of the cheeks of the
air rush deflates and I drop? Nothing.
Nothing is left of my life.

Never never in all my life have I
stood in the basin and wept in
the mirror and turned on the water and dwindled
to droplets and merged myself into the
stream. What will I do if my essence
coagulates, forms into clusters
and sticks to the sludge on the soap? Nothing.
Nothing is left of my life.

Never never in all my life have I
sealed all the windows and turned on the
hob in the kitchen and waited with gas
unignited ignoring the phone
and the door. What will I do if the scratch
of a match strikes a flame that will blast
the whole block into rubble and dust? Nothing.
Nothing is left of my life.

BARBARA NORDEN

The Great Chief

His unflinching lifeless face
points with the purpose of fish,
the profound stern expression,
bloated jowls, roughened skin

like an ageing carp's. His eyes
swell behind thick spectacles
that at dusk he'll remove,
surprised to see us leave.

Every typist in the pool
belongs to him. A large shoal
caught in the sea of hours,
we move our fingers over

the smoothness of keyboards,
touching them like ocean floors
that spread around us vastly.
We breathe currents of air,

a species half-blind, searching
for the right words. I lean
towards the screen and let
my hands create patterns.

But he's head fish. We all
feel numbed by his control
which he exercises coldly,
the still centre in a void.

Because our days are empty.
None have gravity or weight.
Our thoughts must not drift
in deference to the chief.

His office is cool and clean.
Attracted, some stray within
the glass walls. I see his pull
begin and them struggling.

Through the silence, he rules.
His mouth moves very slowly
but says nothing, in a world
where no voices are heard.

ANTONY NICHOLLS

War: a Memoir

1

One day Daddy comes home from the war,
skinny sailor with bright blue eyes,
Adam's apple big as a doorknob. I scream
when I see him, don't know him
from Adam; when he opens his arms I won't
go near him. He's brought us gifts, Donnie
and me: toy click guns, Indian headdresses
he installs on our heads himself with awkward
reverence – it's the first time I've felt
my father's touch. Covertly I watch
his earnest hands, see dark springy hairs
fringing his wrists. Nearby on a table
in sepia, the photo Mama's been talking to
all my life. *This is your father*. Now I see
he's larger and in color; he talks, he holds
our mother in his lap, I see how his embrace
swallows her up, how small she's become
in a grown man's arms. Behind
the big chair where they kiss and hug, I see
Donnie crouched low and shooting
at me. Standstill. My brother's eyes absorb
my stare and in that moment we're the same,
wordless on the floor, heads plumed, guns
in hand, the wounded world at our feet.

2

On a restless afternoon in my fifth winter,
Mama tells us we can look at Daddy's War Book
if we'll settle down. We do. Donnie gets to
turn the page because he's seven now. Side by
side we two pause over pictures of the naked
dead embracing, covered in blood and missing
a limb or two. I'm wondering what holds
a man and a woman in each other's arms
while the world comes down around them. When
my brother finds the last page we see
a row of houses exploded to ash, burnt
baby a burnt baby alone in the rubble, crying.
When bombs fall, Daddy says at supper,
you can hear a kind of howling sound, a slow
whistle as they near the ground. And
so the wait begins: now when I play outside I
listen for that sound. Once, along in our back yard
sucking the forbidden sourgrass, I'm sure I know
I hear it. Breath stalls. I am planted there
amid the sinful weeds, stopped still as a snapshot,
imagining arms around me, a searing sky,
the scorch, the stink, the shrill song of necessity.

3

At Our Lady of the Sacred Heart Elementary
we become Soldiers of Christ, crouching
beneath desks during air raid drills while
far off missiles nudge and shift in their silos.
We pray for the conversion of Russia.
The Sisters of Saint Joseph tell us of a letter
the Pope will open in 1960, heralding
the end of the world, a holy letter

of prophecy handed to an ordinary girl
at Fatima by Mary, Mother of God, while
cherubim and seraphim floated in the
famed celestial lull humming *doom*
doom doom doom doom. Donnie builds
a Flying Saucer Detector in his room. I
buy a rosary, whisper vows and promises
into my cupped palm at night, and
when everyone else goes to sleep
I hear boots in my pillow, bootsteps
of Russians coming
to get me. *I will wash my hands*
among the innocent that I may hear
the voice of His praise. Little girl little
girl little girl STOP. Make it stop. I am
a soldier, years away from having breasts
or kissing a boy but *Please*, I pray
each morning when I wake
alive, *please don't end the world*
till I find the arms to hold
me while your bombs fall.

4
I will go to the altar
of God, to God
who brings joy to my youth:
It's the Summer of Love and whatever
was in God's letter years ago, the world's still
alive and now love is free — people make it
instead of war. Timing is everything: Donnie's
a hippie in San Francisco, learning Chinese
and astrology. I'm a teenage housewife
in San Diego, writing poems while

the baby sleeps. Each night when my
silent husband rolls onto me, it puts me in
mind of continental drift. I feel the bones
bending in my body night by night, hardening
in place, feel the earth tilting toward
a final wordless space. I know I said
I Do, so I did and I do. I had no idea
the world would go on so long.

5
I dream
a letter over and over, written
in God's fine hand, a directive
inscribed in gilt; in every dream
the words are exactly
the same: *Do something. Do
Something.* I wake
to find the world calling
up armies of its young, and
after all, I begin to see. We march
for Peace, we march for the Vote,
We march for Love
in the Haight. Some call it Revolution,
others say it's Armageddon; he's calling
it grounds for divorce. Curve of a
lampshade, pattern of a rug, I contemplate
returning to a burning house. Integration,
Impeachment, Disarmament;
No Nuclear Plants on Fault Lines.
We march for Women's Rights
in San Diego, for Workers' Rights
behind Chavez, get out the vote in L.A.,
leaflet, canvass, petition, boycott, we march.

Off our backs! Viva la Huelga!
No More Nukes! So much to do, so much
to do. We march, we march, we march.

6

I will wash my hands
among the innocent, whether
they like it or not. I'll follow love
where it takes me, with the permission
of the court, never counting the cost
of what is free. I find a man who talks
to me, who knows how to touch, a man I want
more than Sanctifying Grace, and I lie
in his arms at last, his very arms, I say yes
while the Virgin Mary looks the other way
and every bomb in God's Heaven
falls to the sweet earth without a sound.

7

I could SAY something right now
I could TEACH you a trick or two
I could do THAT with one hand tied behind my BACK
ANY man would be tempted to hit you hit you
I could find my way there in the DARK
I could FUCK you all night all day all week all
I COULD have told you a LIE but I DIDN'T
so FUCK you Lady you can see why I HIT you
I can rip a phonebook in two with MY BARE HANDS
can lift you UP with JUST ONE HAND
can drive 100 miles per HOUR with two FINGERS
on the WHEEL I can make my voice HEARD
in a crowd can HEAL you heal you heal you but
I CAN'T take your QUESTIONS, woman

You think too much you THINK too much
I can see why he HIT you hit you hit you

8

My babies, each of them
the only one, wrists fat and creased,
the smell of that downy head – soft spot
of the open cranium, tender brain
pulsing beneath the thinnest
integument of skin – tiny toenails
shoulders and o the smooth unknowing
back of the neck, love, yes, love
without question, new eyes rejoicing
in the sudden shifting of a shadow
on the wall, I took my babies where
love took me, barely thinking
to ask what was in it for them, never
giving them a Heaven or a Hell or even
Armageddon to believe in. At night
in empty rooms now, time hums
a lullaby that measures desire's breadth,
and in the darkness I recall their wrists
and knees, their eyes on me, an innocent
certainty that a mother knows the way.

9

I march again in Cambridge, with
hundreds of middle-aged strangers,
against the War in the Gulf. We take the T
to Boston Common clutching candles, and
there on an icy rise a dozen students take
turns at the mike, but their words
are lost in a January wind that blows

out our candles, too. I'm home
in time to watch the war go on
the news, see they've titled this one
to sound like a poem or a perfume.
There's a hard white moon in my bedroom
window. *Doom*. All night I hear boots,
the boots, in my pillow, I fall
asleep gradually, face to the wall; wake
in my own arms before dawn.

10
In the innocent hours
of morning when robins root
in dewy lawns and cats close in,
in the innocent hours of morning
when the sweet raw air of possibility
can break any heart, in the innocent
hours of morning all over the civilized
world TVs come on for the breakfast show:
The earth, with thunder torn, with
fire blasted, with waters drown'd,
with windy palsy shaken, O would you
not watch one hour with me? Wars,
Donnie, look, wherever you are, see
all our wars this morning, the husks
scattered over land like a trail
of bread crumbs; Are we so lost? Talk
to me. Do we mark our passage this way?

11
We send each other messages
on the internet, Don and I, though we
haven't seen each other in years: *Everyone*

talks about the Millennium, one of us writes,
but no one does anything about it. Ha, the
other answers, *I ain't got time for time*
just now, not sure I've got time for
eternity. He's got a small business in
North Carolina and he translates 14th Century
Kashmiri poets on his own time, follows
the stock market and UFO news. I teach
student writers by day; at night I write
poetry, watch CNN, *Sarajevo Somalia Gaza*
the Gulf again, turn to the Sixteenth Century
English lyric. At any given moment, I can feel
my brother at the other end of the line
leaning over his pages as I am; sometimes
I imagine him looking up from his paper life
at the instant I look up from mine, to watch
the way the world goes on in the dark,
as if moving toward something it could be
sure of, something particular and definitive
that waited at the end with open arms,
waited and listened for our next word.

PATRICIA TRAXLER

Camping on the Fault

A rock broke free and like two stowaways
we camped there drifting northwards on Point Reyes.

One day I left you sleeping and walked through a maze
of pines where I saw a fox which turned and watched me
inching forward, its eyes never off me,
until it backed away into the shade;

which is just what I did when I found you lying on the
    beach
and you didn't see me and your open hands reached
not to wave or beckon me but to catch the heat.

In the dusk I stalked you all the way to the tent.

Like fires on a skyline the eyes of raccoons glinted
from the brush as my own eyes there on the severed rock
looked at you on the other side of the fault
when you eased away, staring straight ahead.

ALLAN CROSBIE

Esperanto

1

The silky skin of the throat
where a kiss left a print, purple-brown
wings. How we kept going back to that place
with our mouths, my first
love and I. The beginners' course
in love and hurt. We wore our bruises
like a privilege, we wanted the world
to know we knew.

There was a life they would give us soon, it was
ours to be studied – the new word for *nipple, erect,*
irreversible, hook and *buckle*, for *when*
and *where*. Alert
as Jehovah's Witnesses,
one foot in the door.

The guide at the U.N. pointed up at the ceiling
of the great chamber: 'The heating ducts are all
out in the open, look!'
No secrets, no war.
We admired the swanky staircase.
We put on headphones speaking
in seventy tongues.

2

A girl's got to think fast, in moves
of one syllable.
In my country, he said, the rooster

says *ku-ku-ri-ku*, the moon's
masculine.

I settled my head
on his shoulder ('Look wilted,
they like it'). You learn
to learn the idiom
when the heat's on.

No chance! No such thing,
he winked. Somewhere
in another country, two people
just like us
are having this very same conversation.
He lifted his glass: *To us*.

3
I'm afraid to. Don't be. Slippery beads
on a string of silences, cool
and glassy to the touch. All the while stroking
my shoulder. And then
that humming like a ground bass, insistent,
beneath the syntax.

Unu du tri kvar kvin ses –
Be sure to
master each lesson before you attempt
the next. *Domo*: house.
Fenestro: window. *Birdo*: a bird.

I wanted to say: 'And after, what if I feel sad?'
but I kept forgetting the word for *after*.

4

All day I'd been waiting. He'd be back
any minute. Soon I'd
run down the hill, brush the grass from my skirt and

walk by, slow, with a practised
indifference. *Hey, is that you?* I tried it out in the registers
of surprise. Too shrill. I sweetened it.
Grass stuck to my summer legs. I kept changing
hellos. If I picked up
the phone on the third ring, my lover

would leave his wife. We would have children,
new ones. I tucked them in, cranky, our own,
and turned out the light.

5

Some other lover taught me the code for
yes: two kisses on the eyelids, one long kiss
on the mouth. Every one of them
taught me. I studied
love. But now

I'm a married woman. You and I are a
man-and-wife, one flesh. *Married*:
you leave father and mother to become

that word. One word
for the hardness that needs to bury its head
in softness, the need that grows teeth,
the feast, the naked cleaving,
the flooding that can't stop itself
and the sadness, after.

6

I am scraping egg from the stacked dishes.
Married. Hot and cold water get married
in the faucet. Still married
and nothing I've ever learned will prepare me
for what I am learning.

You come into the kitchen, buttoning.
Seven buttons, belt-buckle, the chain-mail
watchband. Your mouth
blurs as you come closer.

If I could bring you one clear word
that no one has ever —
I mean, even sex
is a silence
the body translates.

7

Under a baroque ceiling, the Serbs and Croatians
have begun to talk. *Peace, peace*, they say,
and it sounds like *piss*.
They won't smile, they won't look
at each other's faces, they won't
shake hands.

Once they shared a language. A hyphen
married them. *Have a Good Trip with
ENA Motoring Oil* sang the billboards
in Serbo-Croatian, down the coast road
of Yugoslavia. We were still
honeymoon-new:
one flesh, one language.

Now the U.N. translator is seated
in a baronial chair
between the two. Their angers
course through his body,
emerge as words.

8

Our chairs face each other across the room
even when we're gone.

9

Changing planes at midnight, not a syllable
left between us. You doze on a suitcase.
I'm alone, after. In a cramp
of envy, I watch
the Japanese man and Polish woman
find each other

in Esperanto. He's trying out
long and short smiles; she's got on
earnest crepe-soled shoes.
*Hello! How are you! How good
to meet you!*

They're going to save the world
with language. Pure language, boiled down
to the common solubles.
No national epics. No lovesongs. You can't break your
heart in a language
like that.

CHANA BLOCH

The Room it was my Privilege to come down Alive from

The room it was my privilege to come down alive from,
the room I ran upstairs to in the thunderstorm
to where it was impossible to come back down from
without a choir to guide me;
the room where I thought that what I'd found out was
that all I had to do was shut the door,
the room where the bed and the sweets and the door were
    all wrong;
the room in the house like a black plastic sack full of
    starlings
that smelled of sugared almonds and mahogany,
the room where somebody whispers to somebody else
something they don't understand
that doesn't bear thinking about;
the room where you follow the river
and seal the lips I climb;
the room I want to make absolutely sure of one thing
    about,
the room where it was like if you go for the door
he'll get you and chop your head off;
where this one thing is the only thing worth living for,
where this one thing's not even worth living for either,
this beautiful city behind the ruby door,
with all its shimmering supplicants and priestesses
and sweets the size of bedrooms
and bedrooms the size of beds,
and little girls in vests like frightened rabbits

too exhausted now to not be good,
is no more than a rabbit-coloured jelly
spiked with splinters of glass that no one sees,
and no one's going to see,
because it's over;
is no more than a deep-frozen household
enjoying the tranquillity of cold.

SELIMA HILL

Hospital

When you visit me in hospital
Do not bring grapes
Bring me the air that blows into the kitchen
When you close the door from the garden
And the brass knob rattles, as gentle reminder
Of never being mended
Bring me that corner of the chintz bedroom curtain
Faded now with sundance.

Bring me the sound of the dog's quiet sigh
As he sinks deep in the hearthrug
Exhausted in dreamless salivary sleep
A hint of lunch on Sunday: floating aroma
Of fruit from the orchard, exotic herbs, or
Some new dish that you know will tease my senses

The scarlet arguments that flamed till midnight
Quenched by our languid union at the lambent dawn
Bring me the kicking of our unborn child
My hands wandering in wonder
That unforgotten missed heartbeat
When you both went away. Solitude. Rain.
Doves on the windowsill cooing their colloquy

Play me a saxophone which makes pain beautiful
Show me your sepia childhood
In those innocent frilly frocks
Bring me your careless footsteps

In place of that military clock-watching nurse
For I am enclosed now in my own time

Bring me the smell of your body
As we made love
Instead of my disinfected cleanliness

Do not think you can alter my course
But bring the ingredients of the dreams
That will take me away.

J.M. ARNOLD

Le Parc St Cloud

Let's walk to the park: observe the
intervening years cast shadows of
trees on the allées. We'll stroll, and
keep the maiden names of roses
on our lips: Blanche Moreau,
Zéphirine Drouhin, Felicité
Perpétue, Aimée Vibert (syn.
Bouquet de la Mariée).

The fountain is still juggling a
plate of sky on its pole of water:
here's one it dropped earlier,
spiking the gravel with bright
shards. And this is where the
organ grinder ground and ground
one afternoon, unable somehow
quite to get the melody up and
running.

Children are still playing on the
grass. Didier, Didier! The big red
and yellow beachball bounces
away again into the woods.
Let's recommence. Let's
promenade past parterres: their
disciplined ranks of red geraniums
each a clench of flags; on down to
the esplanade, for the fine, if hazy,

view over Paris's haven for
landmarks: there's the
Montparnasse Tower. And no
mistaking Eiffel's shackled
fountain. To the right, Le Bois de
Boulogne, home to whores of
dubious gender. I don't remember:
can we see the Sacré Coeur from
here?

One night on the lawn by this
esplanade, we saw Marcel
Marceau in a marquee, trace
suggestive gestures to a throng.
Cycling back, we were on our
own, two brave little dynamos,
scratching eyes of light out of the
scraperboard dark. We made love
on this lawn by the esplanade, one
June, at dawn, having clambered
in over the wall. Even Marcel
Marceau couldn't match the
expressiveness of your movements
that morning; convey the softness
of your skin in the early light.

These steps from the esplanade,
past balustrades with flowering
urns, that always made me think
of *la figlia che piange*, lead to the
English garden: a willow weeping
by the lake; where we used to sit,
and dream of the stately home

we'd own for its spacious grounds.
There we'd take our ease, our
pleasure; and you'd stroll, on a
scented summer's evening,
snipping heads of roses for your
trug.

Sitting by this lake one evening,
leaning on one hand, your long
hair over your shoulder, in semi-
calculated salicaceousness, you
asked me whether the memories
we make are a measure of our
lives, our loves, our fancies or our
failures. As the light serenely set,
and simulated amber's space of
time, a mallard mocked our
pretensions; and we smiled
together for the cackling birdie.

Up still more steps, and we'll
reach the avenue of trees, whose
leaves went Cézannesque colours
in the autumn. I stamped on them
for their childhood sound. Their
filigree skeletons later dandled the
winter mists in their sketchy
hands. Let's recommence?

If we entered once again by the
gate from the Sente du Nord;
turned left to where the grass was
allowed to grow much longer,

lusher: would we see the tree
through which the light last spoke;
through which the light last gave
itself for us: that blazing
exhalation: streaming out, as one,
as us, from the leaves for the last
time?

DON RODGERS

Mary's Wren

I.M. ALT, BORN AND DIED AUGUST 1996

This morning, early, but August, the sun
Already fierce, Anne is off to the hospital.
I stay home, near the phone, to field the anxious calls.
Inside the car, as she's about to go, she sees
A wren, couched, nestled, clinging to the door.
Carefully, so the little bird comes to no harm
Beating against the car, I lift her up.
She tucks into my hand
Like some kind of home. Her beak gapes
With thirst, stunned by heat, the morning
Air heavy, hills beyond, hazed blue.
I walk back round the house to look
For water and some way to give it her.
I get the garden hose and turn the tap.
The water gushes out too sudden and too loud.
The frightened tiny bird climbs up
My arm as if a branch,
Makes it seem bigger than it is.
Then flies, a step
Away, and grips
The garden wall.
Her beak still gapes, mute and open.
I play the hose straight up,
The water rising, a fountain,
Falling, splashing the wall like drops
Of rain, the bushes wet,

Glistening, and the little wren.
Drops nestle in her wings,
Quiver on her feathers and roll
Like rich transparent pearls.
Her beak closes.
As she revives,
She looks around.
Then flies, not now in fear
From the water's noise, but up, through
The cool shock, to settle
In the great tree, quite near, a tree
With many branches, shading leaves,
Where, from the hard sun and surging
Wind and storm, small birds take shelter.

RONALD TAMPLIN

The Wife

She came to my stall at the W.I. market.
He's gone again, she said.
*I knew it was time when I saw him leaning
out of the window, letting in the rain. So,
while he was doing the milking, I killed
a hen, and left it in the middle of the yard.*

She turned a pumpkin in her hands,
looking for blemishes.
*When he came out of the cow-shed,
his eyes were already round, and his feet
scraped along the cobbles. He saw the hen
and crouched over it, gripping it tight.*

She looked up. *How much is this one?*
It's for my Betsy.
She leaned over with the money. *Well,
and then his wings opened and he pushed
himself up into the wind. Nearly collided
with the barn roof – but he swerved
and then he was away behind the trees.
I'll know he's coping when I hear
of other farms losing their fowl or their
early lambs. He'll be back in the Spring.
I'll hear a thud in the yard and in he'll
come, right as rain, wanting his tea.*

She turned towards the cake stall.
I want some of that ginger-bread for Betsy.
She's a good girl – spends her time face down
on the foot-bridge watching the stickle-backs.
She doesn't seem to feel the cold.

CAROLINE FRANKLYN

Homing Out

It comes back in dreams,
the wide cellar where intrepid steps
took us past coal heap into deep lair.
There were wood shavings underfoot
and, above, floor joists with spidery drapery
thick-dusted and permanent.
Another step down, the great clay mystery
revealed itself, shocking us each time
in the electric gloom: the four foot
terracotta pot with warped wood lid
which slid aside, showed the attractive horror
of bobbing, white, naked eggs.
It was something to do with preservation.

Then there were the stores of table legs;
A rush-seat chair part unravelled
(by Irish aunt's sedentary plenty);
a mattress kept 'in case' and now defunct with damp;
wide plywood duckboards covering artefacts
promised for a rehabilitation.
Over these we crawled to the low inner sanctum
where grown-ups proved too cynic, large, sedate
to venture where the minotaur might.
The laid torch waited to illuminate us;
thence we scuffed knees into secret rooms
founded in the fine earth. There we lived.

Day passed imperceptibly, sun moving unseen
around house above, as we worked in the dim.
Our floors were swept, sifted, the pebbles cherished,
bricks mounted as cupboard, shaped as seats.
Here was a cracked cup, there the scrap-paper
curled in a twilit world and precious as parchment
where records might be scribbled;
and best-loved books, the small, hideable volumes
to be rediscovered and perused by battery light.

Decades later, the favourite hardback will still lie
tide-marked and bent, its blue cover blackened,
pages stuck together with subterranean vapour
and now unturned under the domestic beat
of different and oblivious tenants —
until some new adventurer
follows the thread of secrets, home,
daring the gloaming.

At night I visit in bare feet.

ZANNA BESWICK

How Ducks Happened

And God said
Design me a duck.
I'm offering prizes.

Still recovering from famine and flood, we
    pondered.
Suspicious now of our capricious God
who, we were learning,
liked to play games with humanity.

And then we rescued our drawing boards
from the latest devastation
and sat down to work
in tents or under leafless trees.

What is a duck? we asked.
God faxed us a skeletal specification
– 'It has to float'
'Like a boat, a living boat.'

Another fax came
– 'The closing date's in two weeks, folks.'

There were hundreds of entries,
God dithered and couldn't pick a winner,
so he made them all
and nobody got a prize.

Tricked again, we thought,
as the sky darkened
and fresh horrors arrived from heaven.

CAROLE BATT

Secret Place

(MARY SCHAFFER WARREN)

a. On not reaching Maligne Lake in 1907

It was a hearsay lake – the Stoney Indians
told Jim who told us – our self-appointed goal
for that September. Two ladies, two guides
(Warren and Unwin), ten horses, unschooled
in June, now canny veterans of the trail,
stalked it from the south. After one brilliant

day along Brazeau, storms wiped out the familiar
constellations over our campsite, buried
the track in a foot of snow. The horses'
tails grew icicles. On the third morning
we set off upwards, climbing laboriously through
boulders big as houses, then through meadows
of dying alpine flowers, then among rocks.

The black and white and grey my camera has
    doggedly
recorded in neat rectangles, but I remember
a shrieking wind too solid to breathe, too heavy
to push against, ice-particles like lead-shot.
Glaciers to right and left, and in our faces
a thousand-foot black wall like the end of the
    world.

b. The tale of 1908

The world has shrunk to an armchair in the warm,
pain and puzzlement, ambushes of sleep.

In dreams the clear mountains slide solemnly by,
ledges and levels striped with white. They pour out
avalanches in powdery clouds and waterfalls
that wave in the air like flags of lace. At sunset
doubled in glass their peaks fade through the rainbow
from gold to rose to crimson, purple, blue.

The dream darkens. Horses in bog and quicksand
show their teeth in terror, struggle for life
in swollen rivers. Every precipice
stands by its heap of bones. Thick clouds roll in
and lightning bounds from summit to summit.
Screams stick in my throat. For mile on mile
the blackened trunks begin to fall like skittles
into a noiseless fear. And then it snows.
Men, women and the pack-train slip and stagger
through deepening drifts. Or we wake up to find
the weighted canvas pressing down on us.

I open my eyes, not knowing who or where
I am. Only my husband, friend and chief
guide who shared the shining years, can soothe me.
He holds my hands, knows how to make me smile,
reminding me of the horse that ate my washcloth;
the toad in the tent; the porcupine in the grub-pile.

He tells me a story: how we found the lake.
How, in boots and buckskins, we set out again

with Sampson Beaver's sketch-map, sixteen horses
and a dog, into the untouched heart of the land
up over passes, down through valleys, heat,
clouds of mosquitoes. How, when we were lost,
our dead friend climbed all day to glimpse the lake,
and how we gave his name to the mountain
where he had stood. How we felled the trees and lashed
    them
into a raft. And when we thought we had reached
the head of the lake, we turned a corner
and bay after bay, inlets and islands,
an avenue of unnamed peaks, opened
before our eyes as if freshly created.
And how the warm wind blew the scent of vetch
over our picnic on the flowery lawn,
and our lives seemed significant.
                         Maligne? no.
In my mind's eye it is a blue jewel
drenched in light (lake, sky, Mounts Warren and Unwin
in a bright distance). Peace. Paradise lost.

CHRIS CONSIDINE

Van Gogh in Donegal

I caught wind of change off the Hook of Holland
And set sail for Ireland, a country of potatoes.
I could smell the blight and the skeletal faces
Grown fat on the sweetness of surviving the odds.
They may teach me a lesson about disease
But I doubt it, so that was not my intention.
No, I was searching for diamonds in the soil
Of a starved and dumb country whose language I knew
Only by gesture and colour and look,
And I would fall in love on the island of Ireland.

My puritan soul found no whores in Dublin,
The city was stinking with virginal men
Who'd cut out their tongues in protest against
The temptation of mouths. I renounced paint
And paper and colour. I swear I was blind
To the endearing young charms of girls
And their mothers. I got my comeuppance and happy,
I headed to the very far north. A clarinet
Sea doctored to me. I said, play away
But wash your feet nightly, for like Amsterdam,

You'll sweat like lost souls, and lost souls deliver
Nothing. I found comfort in the whisper of mermaids,
Girls with waves in their hair, hair like red horses,
But in the end they were looking for sailors
Who promised at best a love unrequited.
I became a prophet and preached well worn sermons,

Worn as shoes that stank on my feet, and socks
Were wool and thread from New Zealand, my home
In the new world where I should have gone, but
I travelled north to Ireland, north to Donegal.

The journey was hectic, the food unspeakable,
But reason was my guide, and the stars were logic.
I was a white man in this green country,
So I slept out in the fields and thereby turned green.
Thus I could pass absolutely unnoticed,
A farmer, a tinker, a man without colour,
Yet the treacherous sun turned my skin to yellow,
And for once in my life I was Japanese.
I spoke Dutch to them and they could see Asia,
My words were like placenames from the far east.

Monaghan, Cavan and County Tyrone,
Exotic as Tokyo, Kyoto and Siam,
Places like ghosts, my unforgiving father
Bearing witness to my invisible passing.
I asked for strong drink in the town of Strabane,
I found nourishment in the port of Derry,
A boy let me sleep chastely beside him
In a lodging house, saying I was his uncle,
A priest returned from the foreign missions.
I paid him my Irish money next morning.

Penniless, I hit the streets of Buncrana.
I warmed myself near a blacksmith's fire.
Maybe I washed myself at that same fire
For I was clean as the smith's white beard,
As the white hair that crowned his face.
He battered a shoe and the horse was patient.

The horse was a Protestant, it bowed to me,
I took a Bible out of my pocket and read
The secrets of Jesus Christ crucified.
He took pity and let me sleep in the forge.

Next morning his wife gave me porridge and eggs.
I ate with a hunger I'd never known.
Perhaps with a sorrow I had never known.
I wanted a cigarette after the meal, but
Courtesy prevented me asking, so instead
I looked into her face and thanked her
For lips, for eyes, for nose beautifully set
In the landscape of time. A Dutch word,
Landscape, I said it again and again
Till she turned and walked away. Walked through a
    backyard

Of a house in Holland, of a house in Donegal
Where the back door smelt of chickens and herrings,
Raw herring, raw flesh and fowl, a meal
For the large and loving family, brothers,
Sisters, not like my own. I sang a hymn,
I sang of God's mercy, of horses and sheep,
The creatures of God, He who's protected me
Through life's navigation, who led me to Donegal.
I heard them listening through a window
And my heart was light as a horse's shoe.

I set sail by foot the next morning,
Sure now I could find my bearings, for I was
A sailor and could walk on the water and
The streets of Buncrana were flooded with joy.
I sang the praises of the town clock that chimed,

The Protestant Church and the Catholic Chapel,
I roared with love at the purple Fahan Hill,
I bathed my feet in the lake of shadows,
And shadow I was in the sun of this town,
A foreigner seeking solace from exile.

Why was I in exile? Far from the flat lands? I climbed
Carn Mountain and I was alone. Sight I resisted
But smell led me here, the smell of yellow,
The yellow of whin, Jesus of the gorse,
The sharp Messiah, Saviour of Maoinseah Lough,
Where stories are told of water frozen
And boys and girls skating, like Holland, like home.
Then the ice broke and so one was lost.
I embrace this lost boy as my child, I search
Carn Mountain for the lost bones.

They are not lost, they're in my flesh and bones.
They are purple as heather is purple.
They are flesh as flesh is drowning.
I have lost track of loneliness in Donegal.
I am growing tired of feeling at home there.
I must find a ship and head for the south.
I have a shooting star for a mouth.
When I open it, it speaks of the dead.
Its teeth are yellow and blue and red.
They chew tobacco and spit at the sky.

Still I've known peace on this mountain called Carn.
I'll take the cloth and do no one no harm.
Christ, be my guide through this difficult life.
I will weep at stone and make rock my wife.
But if my red hair were to breed with rock,

Have a child that is silence and dead and mocked,
Who would care what was revealed on this mountain?
Who would care who has paid the price of pain?
I'm leaving this place without sign or trace.
I can be lonely in another place,
Should God choose to call me. I doubt it myself.
He preferred Vermeer, the Catholic from Delft.

T.P. O'DONNELL

The Wild Geese

O the wild geese again! October skeins retrace
their haunted Spring, come back to cry at Summer's wake.
From Limerick twelve thousand purified by loss
moulted old lives, put on spirit-feathers of the flock
took wing to fight for Spain or Louis, King of France
and die in exile, tasting each bitter southern mile
remembering some half-forgotten village dance
some tune or half-in-shadow, belly-churning smile.

Exile – that grave and weighty word –
'Next year in Jerusalem, *shalom*'
Who in our Babel can afford
a curt monosyllabic *home*
whose sense is never twice the same
always another when or where
and every sense a foreign name
and every tune a foreign air?

Yet Spring on Spring, unheralded, the ghosts return
like welcome spirits through a fog, their trumpet
clangour hard and clear. *Lui sans soleil*, a sunless cairn
has covered him and insolent time's oubliette
omitted all his Court. Few now remember
who the Wild Geese were; all that courage and despair
gone like the young, green barley that the wild geese ate.
New words, new smiles, new tunes articulate
new rights, new wrongs. Born to diaspora
no friendly runes for us in bloody viscera.

Startled by my sudden handclap
the great flock rises from its life, up
into Blue (not knowing that it does not die)
multiple creature with a single cry.
The shrinking figure on the quay-side
fades. With nowhere else to go
I stand on exile's rhythmic deck
and watch a single northing goose
go homebound on a northern sky.

WALTER PERRIE

Holding On

We found my sister's grave sunk in the ground.
'3-in,' my father said, and he was right –
a man too old to reckon where he is
from day to day. A bleak and empty place.

The traffic climbed the long slow hill to town –
everybody going somewhere fast.
We straggled, almost nonchalant with expectation.
My mother walked ahead into the past.

The grave was there, cheap marble pulled apart,
as if the ground had trembled from the hurt.
I thought it was the wind caught in my coat –
my earth-bound mother sobbing down the years.

Workmen had laid skewed slabs of concrete on the grave,
as if to keep her in, to keep her down.
She wasn't there. I stood imagining the bones.
My father walked away just like he always did.

My mother never saw him cry; but once
she caught him in the shed, head bowed,
his dirty hands, his shoulders shaking,
putting all my sister's books and clothes in order.

My mother said she saw her on the stairs,
and then she lived with us forever –
a happy, gentle, bookish girl of ten.
She must have thought that all of time was hers.

I watched my father rearrange the stones,
still strong enough to lift and drop and lift.
My mother put fresh flowers in the pot.
And so we left her.

Is this a life? Imagined ways of being,
a few old clothes, bones, and a ceaseless wind;
a girl remembered in a marble cage,
sorrow still kicking after all these years?

DENNIS CASLING

Meeting Gloria

Gloria
Gloria Evans Davies
Where are the poems?
And the murder mystery?
Have you finished it yet?
And the empty farm with graffiti at the end of the green
    lane?
Has it been sold?
And what are you reading?
And where do you get a mop in town?
A proper mop?

I'm reading about the Bloomsbury Set
fascinating the Bloomsbury Set
and the wives of Romantic poets
well they wouldn't stand for it now
and that Augustus John
the way he treated his wives
his sister
she should have said something
going along with it
no good comes of that
do you know after I broke my foot
and my cough was worse
and what with the deafness
I couldn't write at all
not a word
through two winters

then my neighbour Gwynneth
you remember Gwynneth
cataracts they said
brought me lilac dead dead on the stem
but the thought the thought
I shall write a poem called Lilac
but how time passes when you talk of poetry and books
the shops are shutting
I have to take it slowly
but I know just the place
to buy a mop

PENNY WINDSOR

The Last Seduction

'I had always thought Death beautiful.
How otherwise would she get the better of us?'

Marcel Proust

Everywhere, I'm reminded of her . . .

Her perfume crowds my nostrils.
Warm fragments of herself cling to the tints of mirrors
And glow like those faint patches of light
Which come to stay on the walls at night.

She catches the vibration of space
As it adjusts itself around her.
Her lips are so red, they seem always bleeding.
Her eyes enjoy the bewitching blue of light under snow,
her veins the friable blue of cheese.

And when she speaks it is with the long heavy sound
That waves make in darkness,
With the occasional flat note; a blue interpolated minor
    third.
Music which only she can hear.

From a certain angle, the soft folds and contours
Of her body resemble a secret landscape:
Solemn rises and skittish declivities.
Dark nameless places. A recession of beyonds.

Her clothes? Viscous silks. Touchable lustres.
Her walk? A callypygean swank.
With each self-forgetful stride
She burnishes the world still further.

She cries as only a woman who believes in sin can cry.
Every street leads to her home.
The gravity of her warm mass pulls me towards her –
To that nothing from which the universe is sprung.

And, tonight, the moon one night short of full,
I stand out in the open and feel
The wind flow like time around me,
Space warp as from the tug of a dark star.

CHRIS GREENHALGH

A Dream of Gerontius

Malvern, October. Elgar is standing
As lifelike as a statue of himself,
Reading the gravestone with his added name.
Five nights of frost have painted all the leaves
And opened little views of Worcestershire.

The artist of three-hundred, 'Malvern Hills'
Is famous now: 'I couldn't believe my eyes.'

Elgar. England. Elizabeth saying,
'Very pleased to see you here, Sir Edward,'
And the world waits for a balcony scene.

A place of pilgrimage. All churches thrive.
In a manured lane a prebendary –
Cloak, biretta – is smiling and crying.

'Sir Edward, this is Nigel Kennedy.'

His wife and Carice with her white rabbit
Are waiting in a present from the State:
The manor-house is justice done at last.
Its elaborate wrought-iron gates close
With a fourteen-inch gap. Lady Elgar
Believes everyone concerned should be shot.

Visions, miraculous cures, suicides.

The Prime Minister and Sir Edward pose,
Two life-masks, Comedy and Tragedy.

The Chief Inspector cracks under pressure:
'I can't cope with an invasion like this.
Malvern's a national problem and it needs
National resources. I just cannot cope.
I haven't got the manpower to cope.'

Invitations and commissions: Leipzig,
Yale, a Guitar Concerto, Violin,
Cello, Third Symphony, The Vatican.

In Elgar's lane, four Council trailers – TOILETS.

Caractacus besieged with no escape,
Reading the gravestone with his added name.

Malvern on Sunday. The leaves have fallen,
Revealing landscapes of electric lights
And gas-lit pavements on the Elgar Route.
Chimneys point smoke towards the early stars.
An empty train draws in and waits and goes.

GEOFFREY MASON

The Dumb Ventriloquist

His audience was me
and I could see his lips moving.

They let him keep his dolls –
six coffin-boxes in a pile,

jokers who lost their voice
after his tracheotomy,

but when he took them out
they moved their jaws and answered back,

grateful as Lazarus.
The backdrop was wallpaper ferns

and three of his posters –
EMPIRE, PALACE and HIPPODROME.

Jane's varnished face looked cute
and what she said made his face shine.

Cedric the crocodile:
'My teeth are cold, my teeth are cold,

let's warm them round your head.'
'Geroff, geroff,' he couldn't shout.

After the performance
he laid them out and closed their lids

and turned to me that pro
ventriloquist's impassive gaze.

He won't go to the lounge,
'Those dummies gawping at TV',

he won't eat where they do,
a Mr Pountney wets himself,

so they bring him a tray.
He told me evenings were the worst

but still you've got to laugh.
I didn't say evenings were the worst

but still you've got to laugh,
when I left him alone, off-stage,

an air-hole in his throat
and no Jane sitting on his knee.

GEOFFREY MASON

The Master-Builder

Not the birds of the air show such determination:
such a gathering of wood gathering dust gathering
good intentions. Plucked from skips, from hedges,

and the renovation of the local pub, to shape
a ramshackle wigwam in the living-room:
like jackstraws, like a life-sized game of spillikins.

Let these be the foundations, the work of the busy
right hand. Already, it has made out an architrave
and a piece of skirting. It clatters about its duty.

It is sensible. It has things to do in the kitchen.
While upstairs (six planks and a length of string)
the left hand moves mountains with a pencil.

The right hand clutches a screwdriver, the left hand
holds the house in a nutshell.
Love, it says,
I have whittled you an oasis from this empty skin,

from these hase red bricks and black misfirings.
The bedroom and bathroom are nave and chancel.
There will be a lightwell over the stairs where

light falls light-fingered through the chestnut tree.
The walls will be a garden, and the garden
a tapestry. We'll plant quince, crab and maple:

I've planned it to the circumference of the ripple
from the fountain.
In the kitchen, the right hand
extends its sore black thumb. The left hand is a poet.

The right hand has put its head in the oven.
Left hand, right hand, there is no communication.
Between them, rain moulds the bedroom ceiling

with mountain ranges splaying into tracery like leaves.
Between them, the kitchen sink has come adrift;
the house rests uneasily as a fledgling.

Both hands make shift; they take long views of things.
At night, the house lights up like a habitation.
Through the uncurtained windows there are signs

of life: a toaster; a red rose, and in every room
the intricate weft of wood that at first glance looks
something like a cross between a life-raft and an icon.

JANE GRIFFITHS

Lewis Carroll on the Roof

Strictly speaking (of course),
his darkroom's a withdrawing-room,
a retreat (behind the Tom Quad
parapet) from *doing things*

for others (six unmarried sisters
and two thousand-odd letters
answered each year). Precarious:
a black box above St Aldate's

where out of earshot of all
but Tom Tower (with a small
brass hammer in his desk
for children to sound the bell

out of hours) he can justly call
himself invisible. Coaxing faces
from a pool of developer: Jemima
in white, with Fox and a fiddle;

Alice at five; all of the Liddells.
Withdrawing. Beyond *the Reverend
Dodgson*, beyond *Lewis Carroll*;
permanent marks of fixative

on his fingers. But even here
he has rivals. The brief entry
in his notebook for 1873: *today
Alice showed me the photos*

that Mrs Cameron had done
of them: Alice in profile, Alice
at twenty-one. Meeting
Hargreaves in the common-

room: *the husband of one*
I can scarcely picture as
more than seven. Sorting
through old plate negatives –

the sun – the very devil –
playing tricks with the developer;
drafting a letter (*My dear*
Mrs Hargreaves) in the dark

room where long after the last
stroke, the plates chatter
antiphony to Great Tom:
glassy, unstoppable, vibrato.

JANE GRIFFITHS

Hallstand

He would wear sandals with socks,
roll shirt sleeves
back beyond the elbow.

She wore crisp frocks,
blues and yellows, on the lapel
of her summer jacket, a silver
flower-basket brooch,
a gemstone for every bloom.

All summer on shore walks
I'd dawdle, lag behind,
collect limpets and whelks.
That year I was eleven,
changing schools: they'd talk
about my new uniform,
the price of convent shoes.

Odd evenings there'd be a quiet
heavy tone: silence as I'd catch up.

The rest of the summer froze
to a single family snapshot –
I'm standing by the hallstand
watching
as she leaves for hospital.

Each long evening,
bored on the slipway,
I'd tear the legs off crabs,
one by one, throw them back:
smash volleys on gable walls,
until the light would finally go.

The sandals stayed in the airing cupboard
all that summer. And the next.

ANNE-MARIE FYFE

Errata

Page 1, line 8, for incorrigible read unredeemable
Page 5, line 9, for undeniable read indelible
Page 6, line 15, for unreliable read untellable

Dark, and the lights are out in all the houses,
the one streetlamp is swamped in sycamore;
all the hill's houses are cradled in root,
leaves' shadow-selves crowd the walls like ivy:
the dark is laying it on thick, tonight.

Page 16, line 5, for untellable read unspeakable

The cat by the cellar window is a cat-shaped
absence, in black; the cellar window a strip-light
at its feet, a chink: the earth opening up.
The air is sticky as ink.

Page 20, line 10, for supplicate read deny
Page 20, line 12, for deny read supplicate

Suppose the man in the cellar looked up,
he'd just see dark behind the darker spikes
of lavender and rosemary. (The cat is quite invisible.)
And he doesn't look up. He is exchanging words
painstakingly. Dust and ink lodge indelibly
in his thumb; it ghosts to its negative, a thumbprint.
He will leave his mark. He works in the half-dark
almost all night. Letter by letter, he is setting things right.

Page 22, line 3, for jealous read unjustifiable

He is locking up, he is getting a grip on this story
(the press with its oil-black rollers is waiting),
taking the lead weight of it between two hands,
tilting its lead-black against the ink-black
of the window; taking the first, fresh, impression.

Page 38, line 4, for simulate read assimilate
Page 40, line 2, for clarify read uncurtain

The first principle of design is leaving things out,
is in the spacing and the margins. Seven years
is the time it takes for a man's complete change of skin.

Page 53, line 9, for past read future
Page 54, line 5, for amend read alter
Page 58, line 2, for alter read correct
Page 61, line 6, for correct read impose

The lines are unjustified. The errors are spawning.

Page 61, line 8, for impose read query
Page 62, line 5, the bracket should be closed
after the evidence, *not after* as clearly.

The chaise frames the story.
Time and place are composed.

In the room above, a cat tests the floorboards.
It is six o'clock. It is almost morning.
Street-lights turn yellow; the sky comes adrift.
Clouds scud loose and dirt as newsprint.

The house will wake soon. Soon things will happen:
words will be exchanged: irrevocable, unredeemable,
demanding another night's work, and another, over-
    writing.

Page 70, line 2, for unjustifiable read unrevisable

There are not enough spaces between the days.

                                             JANE GRIFFITHS

Patron Saint

Before language, before cannibalism
became fashionable among the better-off,
and folklore a business, before all that
mojo mumbo-jumbo about the living dead,
he was this and that, in many shapes –

Zarathustra, Apollo, snivelling Arthur;
Elvis, Abraham, born-again Prester John.
A whale, a wolf, a wise old snail;
the rumour of a world coming to an end.
He strangled heretics with his one good hand.

He was a wimpish martyr, but mainly a shit-
stirrer, a trouble-maker, a bad-mouthing guru
to cracked poets and quack philosophers.
A lesser god to heathens, hassler of the toad,
the exterminator of the flightless bird.

But before all that, he was a woman
with woman's ways, shrewd and responsible,
a single parent with a barring order
on the father. She gave birth to herself
in the reedbeds and grew up an ordinary man.

HOWARD WRIGHT

Burn

It's there on his skin, etched in relief: neglect.
The half a minute – in which I turned my back,
in which he took his first steps – brands him
forever. He's five now, and tells my friends –
as they half-smile, and adjust blue mugs on
cobalt coasters – what he can't remember.
Reassured by repetition: *Hot tea burnt me,
didn't it, Mummy*. He lets them touch the scar.

What was I thinking, that barren moment before
the squall? Unholy thoughts, damned thoughts.
I was already half-way through another baking –
belly rising like dough, trying to anchor my ache
in the mundane. We were replacing the kitchen
units with antique-look laminate. I was wiping
a spot from the cooker with a green pan-scourer,
and dreaming of your illicit heat. How I longed to burn.

The summer's back – one of our limited stock,
and the scar flashes at me constantly from under
the sleeve of his T-shirt. It grows as he does:
a two pence piece would barely cover it now.
A bleached out bicep tattoo, but of what?
Of a nest of hydras, of a tiny squid fossilised
on his upper arm. Of your tongue, of your fingers
like branding irons, scorching your signature deep.

I knew what to do, about the scald, at least.
St John Ambulance First Aider, barely lapsed.
I held him, screaming, under the kitchen tap, and
he spluttered, enraged by the water fall as I called for
help. From shoulder to shoulder to a central point
at his waist, the skin stripped off his back in the
shape of a map of Africa. Thirty per cent at third
degree. Death was so close I didn't think about you

for two weeks. The crab-walk of your lips across
my pores; your legs, as long and lazy as a punt
up the Backs; the way my flesh melted and
acquiesced. From that, from teabags dancing
under the kettle's stream, to doctors drilling into
his year-old shin, pumping emergency fluids
via his marrow. And his screaming, the morphine,
the skinless savannah of back, arm and neck.

These days, I'm on the look out for danger.
For my son: fast cars, high walls, savage dogs,
shallow pools. For me: still you. My son
stops cycling to pull his shirt over his head
like a razor-clam disgorging: the hot continent
blanched to invisibility. He inspects his arm –
the only significant damage – and pushes off.
He doesn't know why. I hardly know myself.

ROS BARBER

A Farewell to England

Today I said goodbye to Wordsworth –
lowered him gently over the side and let him go.
Sometimes I think I can see him still,
floating like a floppy daffodil just below the surface,
arms like leaves akimbo,
nose gigantesque, fluted, set
in the swell like a refracted trumpet.

Can you tell if this is fanciful
or something else – like crude vulgarity
or loss of nerve or, much worse, indifference?
Me, I'm not sure. Yesterday at noon
I decided never again to write about the Spring
as if it were some universal blessing,
God's kiss in the morning, lambs, new life,
green hope – that sort of thing.
We'd just come through a squall
and Willy was looking green all right,
'Intimations of Immortality' I shouted –
a joke, but I don't know whether he heard.
Green is not our favourite colour.

Certain names are banned – Broughton, for instance,
Easingwold and Clough, Saxmundham, Windermere
and Cerne – all basic stuff but you have to start
somewhere (fell and dale are out as well).
It's the sound that troubles most,
echoing through the mist disturbing images.

Lapwing, loam and Hebden Bridge
are high on my hit-list.

Elizabeth, Shakespeare, Shelley, Keats
were slipped away in shrouds and sheets –
was our bold theme for Friday last, but soon forgotten
because of what happened at the weekend.
(I have dispensed with dates but maintain
the days of the week by declaration: 'today,' I say,
'is Tuesday afternoon' – and that gives a certain limited
   meaning
to the following hours of daylight.) Saturday,
or what I call Samuel Taylor Coleridge day,
was a real whopper of a day,
interesting and memorable for its *disappearances*
when I couldn't stop talking and went
ever so slightly berserk, thinking for one awful moment
that I was married to Dorothy and that Jane Austen
(sneaky boots herself) was coming to tea.

When I came to, the boat was half-empty
and there was blood on my hands – not red, of course,
but blue; and *no Royal Family*
or the Venerable Christmas Day!
And the boxes of metaphysicals, and Donne,
and that palgravia stuff – the whole lot, gone, jettisoned.

Sunday was intended to be a fun-day,
I-wandered-lonely-as-a-cloud-day –
but in the event I got rid of all the beefeaters
and bath olivers, two butts of plainsong,
and a sackful of live madrigals. Then, as an afterthought,
I tossed out Jerusalem as well.

So am I being serious? Well, you can judge:
the crew and half the cargo overboard and room
to stretch your legs and breathe and look up at the stars
to see if I'm on route for the anti-podes; because,
where I come from, it's a constant unmitigated podium,
with everyone from Lord High Podestas
right down to podery editors suffering from what,
at one time, was a pain in the arse
but is now an epidemic of podalgia.

If you've got this far I'll tell you: space
is what I'm after, space and silence;
a place where I can make myself, and then create
a shape – simple, leaf-like, a sort of carapace
or shell for living in; and then a sound,
one small sentence of true pitch, content, form –
nothing less than *Om Mane Padme Hum*, maybe,
but heard, understood, clear
amidst the world's vast meaninglessness.

Is it too much to ask? Well, yes – but all the same
I took the chance to get away
from the podding lot back there, sail south by east,
away from MS-DOS, hi-fi and the CD
of millennium deconstruction, south by east
towards the Jindyworobaks, that long-lost archipelago
where T.S. Eliot is an egg-plant
and Friday says '*étonne-moi, Robo*'.

But getting there will be touch and go.

B.A. HUMAR

Fishing

You left your youth where it was spent
at the edge of the gravel pit, line wet-blinking,
lazy float unbobbing; one hand shooing me home.
The pits now are smoothed and skinned with tar
and new kids fall off their bikes
on the estate there.

And your waters are also
under earth. Stolen at seventeen,
when your skills were just improving
with both pike and
short-skirted sixth-formers.
Our mother joked you couldn't keep your clothes on.

And then she couldn't keep your clothes.
Like a skin sloughed off, they held your shape.
Your scent on the collars planted empty-handed hopes
that you might come through the door at any moment, ducking
and laughing, having stayed out too late. I fished
from the dustbin your hat and your favourite shirt.

Cousins of maggots you warmed in your mouth
and dangled in forced dances before suspicious fish
now swim, hookless, through your socket caves,
bathe in your liquefied marrow. Their dancing
sews holes through your lips, their perverse
reverse darning unpicking the stitches of skin.

You said you would take me out
with tide high, boat black, moon

aching and we would drag in bass
and conger, haul our hull to shore
for sunrise, stretch on pebbles,
cook up saltflesh, boil black coffee.

But even as ice licked the upturned keel
on some forgotten beach, I watched
your fist unfold its bony digits on
the dribbled sheet, the contest over,
will dismissed with honour
in the white defeat.

In my land-locked way, I play
at your favourite pastime. Poaching
recollections others have of you,
filleting them jealously, preserving
them in smoke; I reel in your name
as it reaches my tongue

before strangers; stuff and frame
my disbelief; trawl
through memories, tossing out
crabs, unhooking gills from nylon.
From time to time the grief resurfaces.
Bloated, rotting, but never wholly gone.

Donning your shirt and moth-mauled hat
I search, chapped-handed through the nets,
wind in again and again the sightless thread
thrown out to itch the unforgiving dark.
I call your name to the fish with no reply.
The bait I reel in, always untouched, is *why?*

ROS BARBER

The Long Goodbye

1. The Last Yard
At length Clyde's poets
launch into eulogies in steel
memories sprayed in sepia –
the great legacy of the river
and its tributaries of bunnets

But today in glorious Technicolor
the main gate closes
like a rivet through Govan's heart
the champagne swingers are
missing and nothing can be said

2. Frankenstein's P45
When the steel mill closed down and the men
were told to go to hell
the monster went round everybody to
make his last farewell

He gave two fingers to the customers
who wouldn't use British Steel
He gave two fingers to the unions
and their so-called super deal

He gave two fingers to his apprenticeship
which made his skills unique
He gave two fingers to the government
which labelled him a freak

He gave his last two fingers to the management
and all his mates at work
and rammed his bloody stumps into the furnace
to cauterise his hurt

3. Welder's Lament
ONLY.METAL.
LONEY.METAL
ALONEY.META
.ALONEY.MET
N.ALONEY.ME
EN.ALONEY.M
MEN.ALONEY.
.MEN.ALONEY
Y.MEN.ALONE
LY.MEN.ALON
ELY.MEN.ALO
NELY.MEN.AL
ONELY.MEN.A
LONELY.MEN.
.LONELY.MEN
T.LONELY.ME
ET.LONELY.M
EET.LONELY.
MEET.LONELY

4. Linwood Multiscreen
Dinosaurs
aliens
masked
crusaders
action
adventure

period
drama
enjoy
the main
feature
Behind
in the
shadows
a private
screening
Hillmans
roll off
the line
for the
whole of
this movie
a black
and white
subtitled
short
with no
re-release
date

JIM CARRUTH

To Ireland

In one ear, flute and fiddle and concertina
are crossing to Holyhead on a warm front.

In the other, a viola black with rosin
on frayed gut plays the *Lachrymae* of Britten.

Between: our age's tinnitus, musak
riffling its one-way pack. Poker-faced, I

mask all but a higher strain, cross-strung
in anticipation of the last trump.

*

Catherine's haunt we leave, and Cromwell's
command, leave Popham's curse on Popery

as he hangs Guy Fawkes: now we burn the miles
across Naseby Field and into the Black Country,

quicken our route to where original green
survives and famine is drowned in the swelling

matrilineal ceilidh – the birth of a one
party state, whose single currency is myth.

*

No snakes, no nightingales, and people
in the west who have never seen a tree.

The rules of engagement in a long siege
are clear: once the wall has come down,

no quarter, no words: women and their young
to be shovelled into a church: the flames

like tongues of roasting songbirds, the screams
like skins being sloughed in darkling timbers.

*

A new city, made of words. The quatrains
crowd the pavements, phrases linger

beneath the statue of O'Connell, an image
storms the post-office, and evening is full

of poetry readings. How is it Penelope
has kept weaving so long in the wake

of Ulysses? Suitor now reads Tourist
in a re-Joycean dénouement. Takes a bow.

*

The curse of Cromwell is the knowledge
that we are on this side. The Great Hunger

is with us even after a Full Irish Breakfast,
even after we have driven out in search

of ogham to devour, holy stones and fabulous
tales to swallow. Names are unpalatable,

are old iron rations. Drogheda's pill
still makes us leery, say, of Dun-lay-og-hair.

It is like remembering your dreams –
she remains in the snug of consciousness,

fingering primal cerebellum, weaving
labyrinthine fantasies out of the Book of Kells

that translate into unreprievable sentences
or a never-ending melody of defiant

gaiety at top volume on the penny whistle
in an Irish music pub down by the Liffey.

*

But it is also like a damp squat tower –
Joyce's Martello or Thoor Ballylee.

It is that parody of Maud Gonne waddling
past the Writers' Museum. It is that beggar

whose eyes we threw back, the boy fiddling
a jig for all he was worth, which was

an empty cap. It is that couple last night
ejected from the hostel cursing Catholic and Jew.

*

At the Meeting of the Waters, Moore
is less than the children's desire

to go to Ballykissangel, where English
pour in and pout at a soap bubble from

their bright vale, their purest crystal screen. Time
is paused on the tachograph, but the hills

go on being eroded, as young and old
burst for a first glimpse of what they have watched.

A car-park that closes at 5 p.m. and
a round tower that's pointing to the sixth

century above an unmoved monastery arch.
We march with the rest towards whatever

looks in need of a photograph – some beauty
to rinse our suburban gutters. Here it was

St Kevin came to find his soul's centre,
says the information centre to itself.

*

No quicker way to lose one's soul than
to be in the company of teenagers on

their first Irish Sunday. They swarm
like those bees, Steve, you told me of,

that turned on their keeper when he stumbled.
He swears, then remembers the healing power

of honey. If only I'd some wax to seal
out that banshee down in the f-loud glade!

                  *

A U-shaped valley spreads its sweetness
for us, three hunters caught in the hungry ice

after a day at the Snout's grubby melt
of rock and cool. As our middle years puff

past the perfect replica of a round tower
and a monastery in the Lower Lake, and reach

the Upper Lake, a shag wings vulgarly by
towards the view we're just too late to catch.

Ireland, Ireland, are you all smoky bars
and subterranean shades who let us through

without a ticket, at the cunning word *Finbar*?
Are you all empty barrows? All shells of Molly

and a Goldsmith in bronze? Respectable respect
for the risen word? A credulous reeling-in

of the legendary? This leprechaun you sold me
replies *When Irish eyes* . . . if you press its head.

                  *

The gulls pipe of home, of an inland lake,
man-made, to which I am being wound

by a ruthless absence. Their every raised demand
is an Irish saying, or a fragment of a lost

illumination to a monkish codex
about the exhilaration of the air. *Beware!*

they say. *Only gulls believe they can share in
life on the edge of reason, these wild skerries.*

                    *

I walked out to Sam Beckett's anemometer,
away from the Nibelungen dry-docked anvils

of Dun Laoghaire harbour. There was a warning
about the wake from tourist ferries that might

wash you clean off Rennie's wall, and one
about dogshit. But it was that gauge playing

like a bodhrán at Bayreuth, and Krapp
hammered against the wall with Nobel's power.

The summoning bell for Mass. Outside,
mass virtuality – a football game, guitars,

space invasion, baton-twirlers, and a nun
pausing at a kissing-gate into the world's

largest women's marathon. No peace here.
Dun Laoghaire harbour is not Innisfree

but a gill-net set to catch more shoals for
Eire to drink with, play at, pierce and throw back.

JOHN GREENING

The Day the Grass Came

The speaker is the Norse god Odin. In Norse mythology,
the gods were mortal and knew that there would be an end
of the world, in which they would be killed by, among
other monstrous beings, the great wolf. Odin, the chief of
the gods, went about on earth disguised as a human
workman, and sacrificed one of his eyes in exchange for
wisdom.

1
The day the grass came

I'd climbed to the top of the world
Asphalt gas tip volcano's crater of scum-covered tar
Sloping, slithering, down a solidified lake
To mini-gasometers squashed into rust
Squatting by scaffold bars wrenched into s's and squirms,
Railway lines jaggedly mounting black air
Tangled with cranes crooked over the dangling chains
Clanking on corrugated huts swaying high
On their tracery mounting, clunking on piles
And piles of ladders climbing themselves to confusion . . .
Everything leading to nowhere . . .

Railway sleepers lie scattered . . .

Rotten sleepers lie scattered,
Squirmed in the rusty dust.

Sleepers, waiting for what?

Beauty sleepers, waiting for a Prince Charming kiss?

Sleepers, waiting for what?

For four angels to blow
Rolling the earth in a scroll?

No.
The trumpets and gods have gone.

Here at the top of the world
I sit alone
In my tar-stained overalls
Trying to focus my eye
Over the cities that I advised
As I walked the world in my overalls
Learning how to be wise.

Through me the cities stand
Rectangular, perfectly planned
Tanks of concrete and perspex –
Live tanks, learn tanks, sex-tanks, play-tanks,
Beyond them the work-tanks, make-tanks, think-tanks,
And the tanks filled with monitor screens
For machines to watch over machines.
All tanks connected, computerized.
All tarmac, perspex, one-eyed, and wise.
All constructed by my advice.

Or was this really my plan
When I started to walk among men?

Here in this sacred place
Set aside for the worship of waste –
Olde-tyme rubbish-tip waste –
Not our ever-increasing well-planned waste-tanks
Filled to the top of their towers with plastic cups, memo-
    forms, pay-slips,
Taking their proper place in a well-designed landscape –
But in this primeval place
That dates from the youth of the world
When men drove round in trains,
And I, with my heart full of steam engines,
Thundered to work every morning
In my dungarees and hob-nailed boots,
Shovelled the building sites,
Struggled to get my rise,
Sloshed concrete into the mixers,
Erected concrete silos, where once there'd been silos of
    grain,
Always building for men
Cities with giant-filled windows,
Where men could plunge like fish in clear water,
Like baths after work,
Play with the brilliance of plastic, the glitter of lurex,
Enter dream-worlds of three-dimensional,
Continually realigning, bright projections
In all the colours of rainbow and ultra-red,
With all the bleeps and whistles of sound to add to their
    birdsong and fiddles,
With twenty centuries of the world's childhood
To play with, in many-faceted diamonds
Of view-palace, think-palace, play-palace, dance-palace,
City within city within city within city
Within projection of diamond-faceted dreams.

All this I planned in my jeans and Tuf boots,
Eating my bacon-'n-egg sandwich in the door of the
   chippies' hut.
All this I planned for the beautiful men beside me
Who sloshed the concrete over my Tuf boots,
And built suspension bridges over the Bristol Channel,
Teaching our roads to fly.

On the day the grass came
I sat by the sleepers of the sacred place
Consecrated to the unplanned, antique, waste,
And spat on the ways in which I learnt to be wise.

2

Lord Manager sat on his swivel throne,
Surrounded by switches and thinkophones,
Bouncing e-mails by satellite
To make 'em arrive the previous night.
All the e-mails ever said
Was 'Re your P. As B., take B as read.'
His personal PC stood behind him.
To utter one word he needed a prompter.
'Repeat yourself' – it was there to remind him.
'Lord, Manager, always repeat yourself,
Or they'll kick you upstairs, leave you on a shelf.'
But there's no upstairs.
Upstairs of Lord Manager's perspex think-tank
There's only the sky,
Where all fly-tanks and satellites
Are orbiting round Lord Manager's monitor eye.
For fifty-nine minutes every hour
Lord Manager demonstrates his power,
Broadcasts himself, surrounded by monitor screens,

His picture repeated a hundred times,
His voice-synth message: 'Look, what man has achieved
    with machines –
IN-STANT COM-PUT-ER-IZ-AT-ION.'

On the day the grass came
Lord Manager sat at his swivel screen,
Computerized, synthesized, clean supreme.

3
But just before the grass came,
I noticed one patch of green,
Right at the westernmost edge of the world –
Ultima Thule, last of the Hebrides,
Forgotten for thousands and thousands of years.
One green island had, after all, remained.
One man and his wife, alone.
Congenital idiots, deformed
By centuries' inbreeding,
Yet still alive, seeding themselves like grass,
Living in dry-stone croft.
No think-tank, work-tank, sex-tank, play-tank,
No tabletized eating.
They eat by chewing bagfuls of pounded grass-seed,
Baked with a mildew called yeast
Into brown crusty lumps called bread.
They shit straight into the earth,
Not the deodor bin.
They live as men did when the world was young.
This bent, deformed, ugly couple,
Squalid, and smelly, and old –
No youth-pills, beauty-pills, make-up –
Spend their time crouched over their grass,

Building it dry-stone walls,
Shifting rough stones with their own gnarled fingers,
Dunging it with a few sheep,
Then, all winter, filling a vast leather book
With tiny pictures of all the different grasses –
Green Panick, Sweet Vernal, Cat's Tail, Marram,
Tufted Hair, False Oat, Meadow Soft,
Couch Grass, Darnel, and Tufted Rye,
Barren Brome, Hairy Brome, Water Whorl,
Cock's Foot, Common Quaking, Squirrel Tail,
Silky Bent, and silvery Fog,
Barley, and wheat, and oats, and rye,
Pictured in thin, thin, colours by crippled hands,
Described with spidery writing in faded ink,
Pressed dry and buff on a dust-coloured page.
Grasses preserved in a book,
Grass kept alive on the Outmost Island,
Open as ancient dry-stone walls,
Grass like they reaped in the youth of the world.
Grass which idiots, bent by arthritis
Have tended with ploughs of bone,
Bronze, iron, and steel,
Tended and watched till harvest.

I suddenly saw them, the idiots, bent, gnarled, by no
        means wise.
They have the use of both their eyes.

4
Here at the heart of the world
Lie sleepers crumbling to dust
In a crater of scum-covered tar.

April gusts are frothing the air,
Frothing the steel-wire branches of cherry trees
To pink-'n-white blossom –
No. Cherry trees there are none.
Pink-'n-white blossom is none.
Steep wire tracery, split by the wind like leaves,
Brown fallen leaves of rust.
April's autumn breezes shift the flakes of brown iron.

April gusts are frothing the stream
Into kingfisher-turquoise and red-dappled trout –
No. Kingfisher, trout, there are none.
Effluent turquoised the stream,
Poisoned the air of the tiniest, red-dotted, fly.

But then, slow . . . slow . . .
On that gusty April day . . .
Slow . . . slow . . .
On that gusty April day . . .
Suddenly came the grass . . .
Slow . . . slow . . . slow . . . and then faster . . .

First as green fishes swirling the asphalt lake,
Writhing, and swathing, and turning, and breathing the
     black
Air crawling with dragons of grass clawed up the ash-
     slopes,
Fly-catching lizards of grass flickering over the ladders,
Lightning-tongued grass licking spattering petals of rust,
And spitting out seeds of dragonfly humming-bird
Mayflies of grass spinning over the squashed gasometers,
Flinging the chains, and tossing the sleepers
Aside in a thunder of galloping bison, as rye,

Warm-blooded herds of rye trample over the green
    springing plains.
Days squeeze themselves into matchboxes
To escape from this kangaroo grass.
Terrible seeds bombarding the perspex,
Where the last men cling to their speech-modules.
Time is crushed into wafers.
Grass seed vaster than vulture
Pampas splits skyscraper ceilings,
Peels concrete off like paper.
Years flutter past like oatflakes.
Men flash out of wombs like skeletons centuries dead.

And the grass came,
Riding and mounting the earth
That man had asphalted –
Bullrushing grass, with loins inexhaustible,
Spewing its seed in endless ejaculation.

One by one the tiny museum mementoes
Saved from the childish world in perspex cases
For occasional projection at Histry time on the screens –
Some columns called Parthnun, a spire called Chartker
    Theedle –
Writhed into clusters of tumulent growth,
While the rest of the tarmac and perspex
Smeared over the earth by me and the naked apes
Was kindly bulldozed by pampas and elephant grass.

Here at the heart of the world,
The black chrysalis cracked.
Gigantic butterfly green bright-falconed the air.
Polished the water clear.

There in the pale green stream
I saw my one-eyed reflection sneer
With a yellow-toothed wolf of a smile,
While I felt from my actual eye
Salt stinging tears.

5

Instant Computerization Lord Manager sat on his throne,
Surrounded by switches and thinkophones,
But all the rest of his empire gone.
He bounced e-mails by satellite
To make 'em arrive the previous night.
Now, marked urgent, the message said:
'Re your P. As B., take B as read.'

Take B as red?
Take B as blue.
Take P as blue,
Take blue as red.

Take it as red, as blue, as black,
Take yer red message, yer black message back.

Takitas takitas takitas takitas
Tickyus tickyus tickyus tickyus . . .

Grass burst out of the computer,
Burst through the hundred monitor screens.
Grass like the pounce of leopards,
Grass like the roar of lions,
Grass like the roll of breakers
Crashing the granite cliffs.

'Fetch my administrative assistant'
He screamed.
But with no computer word-pumping him,
His order came out
'Eh aye initat ih-ah,
Eh aye initat ih-ah,
Eh aye initat ih-ah!'

No one was there to understand him.
Red Darnel pulsed through his swivel chair.
False Oat leapt out of his navel.
'Eh aye initat ih-ah . . .
Eh aye initat ih-ah . . .'

His cod-green slime eyes vaporized
To skeleton and marble slab.

'Eh . . aye . . initat . . ih . . ah . . .
Eh . . . aye . . . in-it-at . . . ih . . . ah . . . .'

Last slow echo from submerged speech-bank,
Disgorging discs like seeds . . .

In rushed Chief Scientific Adviser,
Professor Purselips, famed for his study
Of the different intensities in children's urine
When fed on synthesized ice-cream or synthesized jam,
A work which won him the Nobel Prize,
Though the calculations were compiled by his assistant,
And all he actually did was piss by mistake in the jam.
But an e-mail-writer second to none –
Except Lord Manager himself.
The room was dancing with Tufted Hair,

Squirrel Tail, Fescue, and Barren Brome.
Purselips was choking, but made an instant assessment,
Incisively issued his orders:
'Do something, someone,' he screamed.
'Do something do something do something do something
Doosamy doosamy doosamy doosamy . . .'

You, Purselips, you.

You do something. Watch.

Watch.

You, who are honoured with sacred title,
Most sacred title of all.
You, who are called . . .
Scientist.
Knowledgist.
Wisdomist.

You
Have been called
To watch.
To die, watching Green Panick crumble a wall.

Contemplate Panick and die in peace.

Or at least,
Measure the intensity of your own urine
As you panic to pieces . . .

But Purselips scrabbles his itching collar –
Wall Barley rears out of his hair –

Screaming in shriller and shriller and shriller soprano
'Doosamy doosamy doosamy doosamy . . .'

IN-STANT DIS-IN-TEG-RAT-ION.

Oats wave in the perspex penthouse.
Green Panick's phallus reigns supreme.

At last
Earth was avenged.

6
Most of the naked apes died crouched in their home-tanks,
Glazed eyes glued to their view-tanks,
Or hunched in their drive-tanks,
Glazed eyes staring past work-tanks and think-tanks,
Dreaming of home and their own dream eat-tank,
Perhaps a cuddle in their own dream sex-tank,
Or strapped to their seats in a fly-tank,
Glazed eyes glued to a view-tank
Exactly the same as at home
And in all identical homes.

Out of the wash-bins, the cling-film eat-bags,
Burst, like Tyrannosaurus, the grass,
Like fanfares of parakeet, sea-horse, manatee,
Swallowtail, gibbon, and cobra,
Like Bird of Paradise snow white tail feathers,
Like talons of plummeting eagle,
Burst like trumpets, like breakers, the grass.
Like antelope racing,
Like cheetah pursuing,
With all howls, whines, yelps, purrs, grunts, barks, snorts,
    roars,

Squeaks, whistles, and cheeps,
Contained in the marching rustle,
The race of the antelope-cheetah grass.

One moment a million million perspex containers.
One moment Lord Manager's Civilization.
Next moment the pampas
Steeple and skyscraper high.
Every pyramid
Truly grassed over.

Peace, peace at the end.
The earth avenged.

7
There were still, dotted over the world, small beautiful
    men and women,
Who lay down at peace, for oats to breed in their bones.
Men who'd tried teasing ashes for a couple of seedlings.
Girls who'd tried teasing tiny lichens from mould on
    synthesized cheese.
Some there were at whose death I was present:
A wild girl of Brittany, birdsong stroking her hair,
Blown down swift's wings in a swoop of twilight,
Blown down a kingfisher gleam to glow like reeds in a
    whirlpool.
You, my black friend, my neophyte impala,
Corn darting out of your eyes,
Happily washed into wind over ripening mealies.
And you, who once ran to catch at my breath and my hand,
Melt me the mirror, show me death's kingdom,
Tear out my eye . . .
And leave me gasping for blood in the lake of gold,

I saw you blown by the moon through the beards of the
    barley.

Peace, peace at the end.
The earth avenged.

Only the ultimate island
Lay as it always was:
Sheep-cropped grass and dry-stone walls.
Unchanged by unchanging time.
The man and his wife lay dying.

'Our love is a habit like bread.
We are twisted together with thorns.
Silence and space, and your eyes.
Grass will grow out of our bones.
Wherever we lie,
We lie in each other's arms.
Together we've grown.
Together we fall dead.'

8
My time was up.
Out of the thicket that had been Lord Manager's think-
    tank
Came the wolf in his dark-grey suit.
Claws of press-button,
Eyes of laser.

Click went his brain – click click,
As discs flicked – click into place.

Eh aye initat ih-ah
Laughing, he sneered at me,
Grinned with his long yellow teeth.
This is the end of men
After the end of you gods.
But not the end of the earth.
That is the joke of it all.

Not in the spreading dust,
Not in the nuclear ash,
But in gentle, rustling, grass,
Grass, the butler of man.
This is the joke of it all.
The Doom you never foresaw.
You and your naked apes
Poisoned the butterflies,
Oiled over the fish-jumping seas,
Scummed, gummed, down the forests.
All was rationalized.
IN-STANT COM-PUT-ER-IZ-AT-ION.
Here is the consummation
A rational god like you
Who knows how to learn by mistakes –
Oh, I quite forgot, you're through,
Finished, washed out like men . . .
Still, you do have time to savour the joke.
Voilà – the Rationalized World
Waits, like a cordon bleu chef, upon men.
Granted there's no more birds,
No butterflies, no honey bees.
But the useful fruits of the earth
Are ripening fast for harvest:
Barley and maize and rye,

Wheat and mealies and oats,
Bristle-leaved Bent for cattle,
Wavy Hair for sheep –
Though cattle and sheep there are none,
And loaves there are none to bake.
No washerwomen elbows to knead,
No ovens to sniff in the morning.
Still, barley, and wheat, and rye,
Oats, and mealies, and corn,
Seeding themselves across the world.
That is the joke of it all.

That, my dear Odin's the ultimate joke.
Pity you have to disintegrate now.
It's a joke you need time to enjoy.
I alone have the time.
But I can, alas, no longer speak,
Once you, the last intelligence,
Disintelligentify.
What a pity, the joke of it all:
IN-STANT GRAM-IN-IF-IC-AT-ION.
Ih ah ah ih ih aye oh.
Yes Odin, buck up and die –
Aaaaye!
Ih ah ah ih ih aye oh.
Ih . ah . ah . ih . ih . aye . oh . . .
Ih . . ah . . ah . . ih . . ih . . aye . . oh . . .
Ih . . . ah . . . ah . . . ih . . . ih . . . aye . . . oh. . . .

LEO AYLEN

The Royal Charter: Fragments Hurled Ashore

That laden air; sea-weed and beach pebble, torn canvas, cordage,
cliff-edge grass, sea-rocket, thrift and Moelfre's roofs;
stripped spars, immense waves' spray. Their cries and shouts;

the minister, stormed out of faith, weeping
through the six month mortuary of Llanallgo Chapel;
escorting families, Inquirers, newsmen, ghouls.

a lifebelt in Liverpool, *Royal Charter*
faded onto canvas stained a grey
so granite you would never find it now
in all that rock she drove against.

a carved chair in Whitby Parish Church;
part memento, part memorial, perhaps
original, or hacked out from some flotsam
of her timbers, salvaged then, or later.

such alteration: bodies overboard and weighed
with gold (in coin or bullion) sink, not swim.
They stay submerged, caught up in kelp and bladder-wrack

until a sea-change cuts them loose and swells them
to the surface where they drift and tumble in the surf,
ashore at last, where some will know to look.

a legend of the war: the old lady
poured bucketsful of sovereigns
on the post-office counter, amnestied
at last from English accusation:

'this gold-rush wreck, no rescue tried:
the few survivors robbed, or left to drown;
the bodies stripped of their identity
and gold before concealment. Desecration.'

so many years. In each October onshore hurricane
I walk that cliff to watch her come ashore another time;
while villagers risk everything in breakers, on the rocks;

and then for weeks, condemned, deserted, search the coast
to gather all the lost, to lose themselves in action,
lose the thought of where those corpses rise, and rise, and rise.

DAVID HUGHES

About the Arvon Foundation

The fire i' the flint
Shows not till it be struck.

The *Daily Telegraph* Arvon International Poetry Competition 1998 was organised in association with Duncan Lawrie Limited, in support of the Arvon Foundation.

Arvon was the idea of two writers, John Moat and John Fairfax, who in 1968 ran its first writing course. They realised that painters, composers and sculptors all trained by practising their art under the guidance of professionals, but that no such training was available to writers in this country. Arvon was established to provide it.

On an Arvon course, sixteen students, of any age (from sixteen years and upwards, unless the course is devoted to a particular group from school) and from any background, live and work with two professional writers for four-and-a-half days, and write. The course participants must be ready to explore whatever talent they might have. They have to produce, to create. The professional writers set them to work, then work with them. Arvon refers frequently to the Japanese proverb: 'Don't study an art – practise it.' What Arvon courses have always revealed, week after week, is that a large proportion of people possess some talent, given the right conditions for it to reveal itself.

Arvon operates from three houses: Lumb Bank, a large eighteenth-century mill owner's house in a secluded Pennine valley outside Hebden Bridge in West Yorkshire; Moniack Mhor, a converted croft house and extensive stone outbuilding overlooking a commanding Highland landscape, fourteen miles from Inverness in Scotland; and Totleigh Barton, a farmhouse dating from the eleventh century, near Okehampton in the middle of Devon.

Two-thirds of the writing courses are open to the first sixteen people who book on to them. The other courses are organised for schools and colleges, for teachers of English and teacher trainees, and for other specific groups. It is a firmly held principle of the Arvon Foundation that its courses should be accessible to anyone with a serious interest in writing, whatever their financial means, and a Bursary Fund has been established to support those who are unable to afford the full course fee.

Lord Gowrie wrote: 'Arvon's influence on the literary life of the country has been and continues to be immense.'

If you would like further information about the Arvon Foundation and its writing courses, please contact:

> David Pease, National Director
> The Arvon Foundation
> Lumb Bank, Heptonstall
> Hebden Bridge
> West Yorkshire, HX7 6DF
> Telephone: 01706 816582